Chris Hirst is Global CEO for Havas Creative Network, a multi-disciplinary marketing services network. Once an engineering graduate working in a glass factory, his career path has taken him to the boardroom via Harvard Business School. Named in 2018's *Evening Standard* Power 1000 list and ranked one of the industry's most influential CEOs, Chris is a regular speaker, presenter and commentator in national press including BBC News, The Politics Show, *Evening Standard*, CNBC, *Financial Times* and Sky News. His podcast in partnership with Intelligence Squared is available to download now.

For updates visit *www.nobullshitleadership.com* or follow him on Twitter *@chrishirst*.

T0124536

No Bullsh*t Leadership

Why the World Needs More Everyday Leaders and Why That Leader Is You

Chris Hirst

P

PROFILE BOOKS

This paperback edition published in 2020

First published in Great Britain in 2019 by
Profile Books Ltd
29 Cloth Fair
London EC1A 7JQ

www.profilebooks.com

5 7 9 10 8 6

Printed and bound in Great Britain by
CPI Group (UK) Ltd, Croydon CR0 4YY

A CIP catalogue record for this book is available from the
British Library.

ISBN 978 1 78816 253 1
eISBN 978 1 78283 545 8

To Ann, Dylan and Sam

All men dream: but not equally. Those who dream by night in the dusty recesses of their minds wake up in the day to find it was vanity, but the dreamers of the day are dangerous men, for they may act their dreams with open eyes, to make it possible.

Seven Pillars of Wisdom, T. E. Lawrence

CONTENTS

Foreword by Sir Clive Woodward   1

Introduction   4

1 Are you a leader?   9

2 Leading to where?   14

3 How to get there: being decisive   27

4 Culture   54

5 Being followed   94

6 Energy and resilience   130

7 Leading yourself   147

8 Leading change   171

9 Conclusion   206

Selected further reading   210

FOREWORD

Sir Clive Woodward

NOBODY IS A BORN leader. However, it is something you can learn and develop in yourself, and coach and teach in others. Many assume leadership ability to be determined by personality traits such as self-confidence, charisma and certainty of vision, but in my experience, the two most important skills effective leaders possess are things we can all do – if we choose to. The first is to be really good at listening, and the second is to remain permanently curious, open and willing to learn. The days of a remote leader that only very senior people get to speak to are over; everyone today expects to have a voice and be heard. More than ever before, today's successful leaders must be able to listen effectively and learn quickly.

Great leaders recognise that the best ideas won't only come from them. It's not a matter of 'ceding authority', you're still going to have to take responsibility, say yes or no, but great ideas can and will come from everywhere – if you let them. I have never thought that I was particularly good at ideas, but I am good at creating teams that are able to think for themselves. And I'm very good at listening and acting on what they tell me.

I have also always loved to learn. Not just from my

own experience, but from others – whoever or wherever they may be. I will travel anywhere in the world for the opportunity to understand or uncover something that may make me a better leader and coach. Once you view learning as part of your job, you'll be amazed at the breadth and variety of people who can teach you something new. I call this 'relentless learning'. When I was head coach of the England Rugby Team on our journey towards the 2003 World Cup we experienced our share of famous victories and unwelcome defeats – as all teams do. However, instead of simply celebrating our victories and spending many hours mulling over our defeats, we did the opposite. We brushed off defeats as an inevitable (if unwelcome) part of the job; when they came along we had a beer or two (you still could in those days) and put them behind us. However, when we won, we were determined to learn from it; we were in early the next morning deconstructing what it was we had done right and made sure we were even better next time.

If you are a good listener and a quick learner, then you are well on your way. With these two ingredients, leadership may turn out to be much less complicated than you thought.

I first worked with Chris nearly ten years ago when he was the newly appointed CEO of a business striving to shake off a terrible reputation and with recent performance to match. He approached me because he rightly believed we shared a restless desire to learn, a passion for trying new ways of solving familiar problems and a healthy disrespect for bureaucracy, pomposity and received wisdom. That is how I've found him ever since. He is as the title of this book suggests.

Chris is one of the most unconventional and successful leaders that I know and this book is about how he works. He's a great listener and you see here why people enjoy working with and for him. He is, as I like to put it, a sponge rather than a rock. Like all successful leaders, he is tough and driven, but never lets you forget that ultimately leadership is about people and what comes through on these pages is the warmth and humanity with which he approaches his role.

Every page of this book is bursting with thoughtful, yet practical advice, all tried, tested and proven. It is no ego-driven list of achievements, but an honest account of the difficulties, failures and tough choices that are necessarily part of being a leader. And how through clarity of thought, working to develop your own leadership skills, and focusing on action, you too can overcome and succeed.

Leading is about relentless learning and I unhesitatingly recommend this book to anybody who wishes to improve their skills, effectiveness and successes as a leader. No matter who you are, what kind of organisation or size of team you run, there's something here for you. So good luck – and trust me, after a couple of hours with this book, you may find it's not as difficult as you think.

INTRODUCTION

I HESITATE TO WASTE my time and yours on yet another book about leadership. Yet never has the subject been more important. We look around our world and see millions of people yearning for leaders who can help them fulfil their potential. We need better leaders everywhere, in politics, science and business, in our schools, hospitals and prisons. Where are the great, if often flawed, leaders of the past? We live in a time where people (and particularly, but by no means exclusively, the young) demand leadership by consent, yet paradoxically we see, in our public life at least, the return of the demagogue.

Leadership has become a word devalued by over-promise and underdelivery, by the waffle of business schools and business books, by the perceived failings of politicians and businessmen (and women). This bullshit that surrounds the subject both inhibits people from fulfilling their potential and excludes people from believing they too could lead. Leadership is a word drowning in words, crying out for rescue.

We need not a new word but a new understanding, one that illuminates rather than obscures, includes rather than excludes. We have always previously believed that leaders are the people right at the very top of our public life: politicians and CEOs; generals and dot-com billionaires. This is who business schools and business books speak of and to when you open their covers. However, important though these people may be, they are the 0.0001 per cent; few of us will ever even meet them, never mind actually join their club.

The reality however, is that today, millions of us are leaders: whether you run a hospital ward, a weekend football team, a high school department or a thirty-person start-up. Most of us will never have a Harvard Business School case study written about us; but anybody who has people who depend on them is a leader.

Our complicated and interwoven societies are full of everyday leaders just like this, and it will enrich all our lives if greater numbers amongst us not only recognise the leadership opportunity we have, but also feel more confident and able to grasp it. And in doing so, thrive. Not everybody is a leader and not everybody wants to be, but many thousands are and each is striving to fulfil their own lifelong ambitions, worrying at night about how they're doing and agonising about the successes and failures of those who rely on them. These are the leaders who make our societies tick and outnumber millions-to-one the subjects of business school case studies.

Not only are leaders all around us, but the hierarchical world we grew up in is disappearing. Old-fashioned, top-down management is becoming less effective and less relevant across our societies, in our companies and even in how our countries themselves are run. It doesn't work because it is too slow, too unresponsive and too one dimensional; it doesn't work because it restricts rather than liberates the power of the whole team; and it doesn't work for the simple reason that people won't put up with it. Today, as never before, people expect to have a voice, have a say and be listened to. Leaders at all levels must build cultures that encourage people to speak up and out, and respond effectively and inclusively when they do. We can only achieve our collective potential by unlocking the potential of the hundreds of thousands of leaders in our midst.

All of our futures rely on more, better leaders, leaders who already exist in all walks of life: everyday leaders. This book is for these people.

I have been a leader for the majority of my career, although for many years I, like most people, didn't think of myself in that way or even recognise that as my role. At first I ran small teams of two to three, and today I run a business that spans the globe with over 8,000 people and more than eighty offices. It was only around ten years ago, however, when I first became a CEO, that I began to think seriously about what leadership is and how it can be done well – or badly.

I had become head of a drab and failing advertising agency – one that had stubbornly resisted change despite the efforts of successive management teams, some of which I had been a member. Through the years of failure I had seen that good intentions, hard work and smart people, though essential, were not enough. Now I had my chance, but would it prove a poisoned chalice; was the business unfixable? Nothing was certain about the journey ahead other than I was determined to both learn from, and never repeat, the many mistakes we had made to that point, and in doing so I began to consciously learn to lead.

This book, then, isn't a theoretical discourse – consider it more a manual, built on the back of meetings, conversations, weeks and even years where I fucked up, avoided difficult choices and trusted in the wrong people. My hope isn't that you don't fail: periods of failure are inevitable, and acceptance of this is a liberating state. Rather, my hope is that by cutting through the bullshit that surrounds leadership and being able to focus yourself and your team on what matters most, your victories will rapidly exceed your defeats.

So how does this book work? First, I'll tell you what I think a leader is, and you can decide if you are one or want to be one. If so, we'll begin. We'll explore a new and very simple definition of leadership: that it is simply the getting from one place to another. The first task of a leader then is to agree and decide where you are leading people to. I'll show you how to get them there, and how making better, faster decisions and re-framing your fear of failure are essential to this. A leader must be followed. We'll look at how you build the team you need around you, and the culture that binds you together. Of course, you can do all this perfectly and still not reach your intended goal. We'll look at the importance of maintaining the energy of your team throughout the journey, and how this is impossible if you are not effectively managing yourself. Finally, we look at the hardest situation of all: how to turn around a team that is broken and failing. I'll show you that the rules then remain as simple as before, but putting them into practice gets harder still.

*No Bullsh*t Leadership* does what it says on the cover. It clarifies and simplifies, stripping leadership down to its most basic components, leaving the reader with a framework on which to construct their own leadership philosophy and style. It is as long as it needs to be and no longer; treat this book with disrespect, scribble on it, fold over the corners, tear out the pages; steal from it, improve on it, wildly disagree with it, lend it out and snatch it back. Use it.

Most of all, this is about how to get stuff done, and if you're like me you have no time, short attention and want it straight, no bullshit.

1

ARE YOU A LEADER?

A short pep talk to the waverers

*If your actions create a legacy that inspires others
to dream more, learn more, do more and become more,
then you are an excellent leader.*

Dolly Parton

I'M PRESUMING THAT IF you've got this far you're either standing around in the airport bookshop, filling time because your flight is delayed, or you've taken the plunge and decided to give this book a go. In either case – thank you.

Before we proceed, however, a health warning. If you're looking for long words, nuance and complexity you've come to the wrong place. You'll get none of that here. Quickly close the book before the spine is broken and take it back.

In both cases you have made a conscious decision to pick up a book on leadership. Therefore you have at least a passing interest in what leadership is, and a desire to improve your leadership skills. Perhaps some of you are asking yourselves if you are a leader at all. I hope that's the case, because you're exactly the people we need: anybody who has neither self-doubt nor desire for self-improvement is both unlikely to be reading, and, in my experience, unlikely to succeed.

You'll work out, as you skip through the following pages, that I have little to add to the vast store of research on trying to define a 'leadership type'. Not only do I consider this to be a waste of time, but worse, it can perpetuate the exclusion of certain types of people and groups from leadership positions.

It sadly remains the case that some parts of our societies, for a whole load of well-documented reasons, find it easier to get into leadership roles than others. It is an incredibly important issue and one whose depth and complexity goes way beyond the scope of this book, but its resolution is of the highest moral and economic importance. These societal factors, that of course we need better leaders to help us fix, must not be confused or obscured by erroneous attempts to make leadership the preserve of certain personality types.

I can't change society with this book, but I can create better, more successful leaders, because 'leadership' is a muscle that can be trained and developed. The good news is that in my practical experience there isn't a 'leadership type'. What this means is, it could be you – indeed, it may already be you. You just have to recognise it and grasp it. So here goes.

A leader has both authority and responsibility. The inverse makes the point even more forcefully: without both authority and responsibility one cannot be considered a leader, irrespective of title or position.

No one is born a leader, and the process towards leadership is uneven. For many people it is a long journey, and for some it is unasked for. Sometimes a leader finds herself the unwilling recipient of responsibility and must decide whether she wants to take it. Our cultural histories abound with stories of the unwilling leader forced through chance and adversity into the role.

More often, in our real, day-to-day world, the nascent leader has the choice: to take up their authority, or not. At different times all leaders will find themselves at this point. Typically, it is when we find ourselves in a new role – for example, when we raise our hand at a community meeting, agree to coach a kids' football team or when we get promoted. It can be a moment of mixed emotions: celebration, exhilaration, trepidation or perhaps even anxiety. Whatever your feelings, it brings with it new and often significant challenges.

At some point, promotion means the unavoidability of leadership. For even the most confident people, these are moments of great personal challenge and self-doubt, even if we choose not to admit it. The successful leader would be wise not to wait until this moment to consider what that means in practice, and how she will respond. Leading is not just a slightly bigger job; it is a completely different job. Here is where the thoughtful and serious leader should begin to consciously learn their craft.

A leader at whatever level must be prepared to take up their responsibility. To some it comes naturally and without thinking, to others it doesn't. This makes one no better or more 'natural' than the other; they are just different. In fact, I could convince myself that those who choose to think about and consider their leadership style are the kind of leaders we need more of today. This book is designed to help with the practical process of learning and everyday leading.

We can all be leaders. Maybe not everybody wants to be one, but that's different from not being able to do so. A former boss of mine, Richard Hytner, wrote a great book called *Consiglieri* about the enduring power of the No. 2. I would argue, however, that this is simply leadership under another name and in a different guise. No matter your position in an organisation, if you have people you're looking out for, then you're a leader too.

We can all lead if we choose to. What follows, in my opinion, is how.

1

ARE YOU A LEADER?

Anybody who has people who depend on
them is a leader.

Our societies, businesses and communities need
more and better leaders from all walks of life.

Top-down, hierarchical leadership doesn't work any
more: we need a new way for new people.

The bullshit that surrounds the subject of leadership
both inhibits people from fulfilling their potential and
excludes people from believing they too could lead.

No one is born a leader. There is no leadership type.

We can all lead if we choose to, and what
follows is how.

2

LEADING TO WHERE?

The most effective way to do it, is to do it.

Amelia Earhart

Leadership is difficult, but not complicated

Leadership is simply the getting from one place to another.
I've drawn a diagram to help:

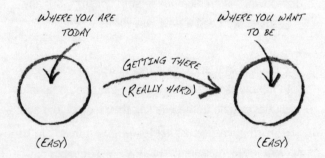

It didn't take me ages, nor should it have. But there
is a serious point here, and it does deserve a little
elaboration:

Leadership is the activity concerned with the navigation of a group from a defined starting point in the present to a different, clearly and simply defined state that exists in the future.

Much is written about the subject of business change, but in reality all leadership is about change. By definition, leadership cannot be about the maintenance of the status quo. As the Red Queen explained to Alice, 'Now, here, you see, it takes all the running you can do, to keep in the same place.'

So to lead, you first of all need to know just two things, and it is here where so many books on leadership start to make it all so intimidatingly complicated.

Step 1: Define your starting point – keep it simple and be honest (even if it's painful)

To begin a journey you have to understand your starting point. In practice, this is often a trivially easy question, with an essentially uncomplicated answer. Frequently, people mistrust answers that appear to be simple or obvious. Don't. Always start with the simple and obvious, because very often that's what things are.

For example, you may evaluate your team's performance in financial terms or by points gained, in terms of patient outcomes, staff turnover or awards won. In many service sector organisations Net Promoter Scores are increasingly used as an almost real-time measure of team performance (usually this is the answer to a single question, such as: 'How likely are you to recommend organisation X to a friend or colleague: score 1–10'). Typically (although by no means always) success is measured relative to your competition or other third parties (in the public sector performance leagues are common, for example). Likely, the answer will be some combination of hard measures (being tangibles you can physically count: such as exam results, wins or sales) and soft measures (being intangibles: such as survey findings or customer satisfaction).

However, measures such as these never tell the whole story. You may discover that you have unhappy customers, but you need to know why. To do so you must look inside your organisation. The easiest way to find out about its strengths and weaknesses is to talk to people who have direct experience of what's going on at ground level. It has long been observed that a short conversation with somebody who works on the checkout at a retailer would be enough to give you a pretty accurate idea of the challenges that business faces, and what might be needed to fix them. Many millions of lines of business school and academic theory have been dedicated to this approach. Read them if you're so inclined and have the time, but the sentence above pretty well covers it – just find your equivalent people, make it safe for them to be honest (we'll come to that later) and really listen to the answers.

An effective way to do this is to fix round-table meetings with a representative cross-section of people and pick their brains – when I had BBC Radio 1 as a client they used to call these 'pizza meetings' (free food always helps). In large or decentralised organisations anonymous online surveys are a very fast and cost-effective alternative (although face-to-face is definitely preferable). Customer-facing or front-line staff are always particularly insightful (cashiers, nurses, teachers, flight attendants or call centre staff, for example). You'll discover that all organisations look very different when viewed from the bottom up. The trick is to talk to people who will have an opinion based on their day-to-day experience and (at least some of whom) fall outside the circle you would ordinarily interact with – such as your direct reports.

What is important is that you don't mistake a simple definition of the problem with there necessarily being a simple solution to it. Solutions rarely are, but we'll come to that.

Step 2: Define your end point – keep it simple

Once you've established where you currently stand, the next step requires the slaughtering of one of the sacred cows of business strategy – the fetishisation of 'visions' and 'missions'. The language around 'visions', 'missions' – and there are many more, for example 'Big Hairy Audacious Goals' (BHAGs – yes really) – is increasingly part of leadership orthodoxy. In reality however they, and their accompanying books, videos, lectures and method-ologies, are just variations on ways of asking, 'Where do you want to get to?'. Or even more simply, 'What's your (leadership) objective?'.

If there's one section of this book I urge you to pause at and think through, it is this one. Theorists might violently disagree – but I'm a practitioner. My contention is that my way is faster, easier and more liberating. And you don't need to pay a consultant to help.

The problem with 'visions' is not that they don't matter, it's that so often the leader's quest to define their 'vision' becomes a destination in itself, a quixotic search for uniqueness and eloquence, whereas in reality, defining the destination for your team is not that difficult, and you shouldn't treat it as if it were. Yet the massive Leadership Industrial Complex that exists around the definition and the selling of the process, theory and language around company 'missions' and 'visions' has convinced almost everyone that this is the most complicated, important and defining of leadership tasks.

Once upon a time I too was persuaded that this was the case. Now I'm convinced not only that much of this is just bullshit, but worse, that the grand claims of this industry often actively stifle and intimidate leaders into never being able to start on their journey at all.

I'm here to tell you to kill that sacred cow. Liberate yourself from the tyranny of the orthodoxy. Once you do, you'll be surprised how fast you'll be able to progress.

But how?

You can do so by returning to the question: Where do we want to get to?

This question is all you need. Of course you're free to make the answer to this as complicated as you like, but I urge you to keep it simple.

In 2015 England staged the Rugby World Cup. England has one of the world's richest rugby unions, with a very well-funded team and a huge player base, but the team was humiliatingly eliminated in the first round. It was the first time in the competition's history that this had happened to the host nation. The coaching team were fired and a new head coach, Eddie Jones, was appointed. He found himself faced with a version of my two questions.

Q1: Where are we today?
A1: Humiliated, defeated and broken – a generation of players scarred by a career-defining experience.

So far, so obvious.

Q2: Where do we want to get to?
Eddie's answer: We want to win the next World Cup in Japan in 2019.

That's it.

He could have waffled on about inventing a new form of rugby, or making the nation proud, or culture, or values, or youth, or any of the other things sports teams and organisations talk about endlessly, but he didn't.

We want to win the next World Cup: it's obvious, it's clear and it's liberatingly simple to understand.

How to get between the two points – well, that is the very, very difficult bit.

This is where leadership happens.

Many leaders, in reality, never even get to the actual task of leadership, so lost do they become in trying to find intellectual and clever answers to these two questions. Consultants make a very large amount of money from helping leaders find these complicated answers. It is almost as though they see leadership as being about defining mission statements. It's not.

As well as often being a fruitless task, the result of these endeavours is a 'vision' that in reality is impossible to execute, and is complicated and difficult for the organisation to understand in the first place, let alone remember.

Ask yourself if you have ever run or been part of such a process and how often. Furthermore, of all those thousands of hours, how much of what came out ever made any difference at all – or ever had any meaningful existence after the end of the process? If you're honest, not much at all.

So why do we persist?

Finding simple answers

There is an easier way, and that is to search for easier answers, answers that you and your team can readily understand and buy into. Very few companies have a unique product or service, and yet many persist in trying to find a unique way of defining themselves. Hence the ever-more tortuous or highfalutin language that comes from such sessions. For almost all businesses the objective is not to be unique, it is to do a common thing better than the competition. This should be the objective. If your company has a unique position or even an opportunity to be unique, grab at it, but don't attempt to invent it if it isn't there.

Ultimately, the answer will be driven by you, your

team and your own particular circumstances. Objectives can range from the inspiring and ambitious, such as Southwest Airlines' 'Democratizing the skies' to the no less ambitious, but more functional, 'to win the World Cup'. Neither approach is better than the other, nor is there a right or wrong; you and your team must find your own answers. Leaders may be responsible for setting objectives for entire organisations (such as the two examples already given), but for many more of us, they will be based around the needs of our department, or our team. We could wish to top an internal sales league, a sports team may aim for promotion to a higher league, a school to improve its OFSTED rating, a charity to improve its fundraising – or perhaps, heaven forbid, just aim to all be happier and more fulfilled.

The objective of this book is not to tell you what your solution might be, it is to encourage you to stick to some simple rules to make sure your answer has resonance and meaning to your teams and avoids sitting unread and discarded on dusty shelves. That in the final analysis, it is something you can act upon, something that facilitates and liberates, rather than, as is so often the case, looking pretty on the page, but ultimately getting in the way of progress.

A great example of the power of clear, simple and actionable objectives are learning objectives – now standard practise in many areas of teaching. A learning objective can define an entire course (and then be broken into actionable steps) or a single lesson. For example, a learning objective may be: 'to create a social media marketing campaign for an organisation' or 'to determine the most appropriate exercise for health maintenance in elderly patients'.

Education resources website theschoolrun.com suggests that every primary school lesson should be designed around a learning objective, which it defines as 'what the teacher wants the children to have learnt or achieved by the end of the lesson'. This is translated into the more child-friendly acronym WALT (We Are Learning Today) and written clearly on the board at the beginning of the lesson. The learning objective provides direction and comprehension – it guides the teacher in shaping the discussion and helps explain to the kids why they are doing what they are doing. By definition it should be simple (although not necessarily easy), measurable and be clearly understood by all. Measurability allows teachers and students to log their progress. Examples of lesson objectives might be, 'to be able to multiply two two-digit numbers together' or 'to be able to write a description of a setting for a story'.

If you're finding your team hard to lead, imagine having to herd a group of unruly eight-year-olds towards their lesson goal. An effective learning objective allows teachers and their pupils the space to discuss and explore a subject without losing track of the eventual objective. The parallels for all leaders are, I think, obvious.

Defining your objective is not easy; it is an exercise that can be difficult to do well. However, don't let yourself believe it is *that* difficult – and it's certainly not as difficult as what comes next (actually having to get on and do it).

To return to the teaching example, I know I would find designing an entire course difficult, but the prospect of actually then having to deliver at the front of the class is terrifying.

As with learning objectives, you should ensure that you keep your answer simple, realistic and easy to understand. It must be a constant touchstone for you and your team. It must help the process of decision-making and give a clear sense of what to prioritise and what to drop. It's obvious, but necessary, to remember that it must also be clear whether, over time, you are getting closer to fulfilling its ambition. A great objective, as well as being a common point to aim for, also liberates and energises your team – thus making the achievement of the goal that much more likely. You too will most likely need to break it down into stages of activity, exploration, learning or investment. And of course, allow for plenty of back-tracking when some things don't go as planned.

For example, you might just say, 'We are going to be the best.' This approach polarises. A blog I wrote on this subject divided readers into those horrified by its nakedness and lack of higher purpose, and those who applauded its simplicity. Whatever your view, it fulfils all my criteria: it's easy to remember, it's competitive, it encourages transformational solutions and, ultimately, if you get there, you win. To me, it's an effective and bold goal. I'm surprised how many shrink from similar bold approaches. Maybe it's easier to hide behind floral language.

You may decide to be the biggest, the smallest, the

fastest, the most nimble or have the best customer service. You can focus on the experience of your employees or your customers, or your organisation's place in the world. Or, as is increasingly fashionable, you can be purpose-driven. You can think medium-term or very long-term. What is most important to remember is to focus on what works for you, your team and your organisation. Too often leaders fall into the trap of doing the thing they think they *ought* to be doing – rather than staying laser-focused on the thing(s) they *should* be doing, that will be most effective most quickly. It is this dissonance that so often derails leaders at this stage.

A politician may think, 'How do we win the war?', but a general sees only a series of campaigns and battles, each one with unique challenges and objectives, requiring different strategies and tactics. Both require leadership, objectives and action to achieve their goals, but both must approach their tasks in very different ways and against very different time frames. The leader must also consider his or her place in the greater scheme and consider their goals, strategies and tactics accordingly.

If your operation isn't unique (which it almost certainly isn't), your goal is to *outperform*. There are an infinite number of ways, styles and philosophies that may define your end point, but whatever your answer, always search for simplicity.

To be the best

Let's briefly return to the word 'best'.

I like this word.

I like it for two reasons. First, I love its ambition. It's incredibly hard to do, but if you're the leader, surely that's your job. Secondly, done right it forces you to be revolutionary rather than evolutionary. Aiming to be better leads to incremental changes. Aiming to be the best forces rapid and dramatic change.

I believe the reason that 'vision' and 'mission' statements often avoid words such as these is because they seem both too simple to define and too scary to commit to. They do not appear to be intellectual enough and they set a very high bar. Yes they're scary, but that's the exact reason I love them.

Another criticism I often face with this approach is that it is necessary to define what we mean by the best, the biggest, the fastest, etc. Back to the task in hand. The leader's primary objective at this point is to define direction and ambition. If you set your team the challenge to be the best in your organisation, then once you get close (top three, for example) it might be a good idea to refine your definition. But in the meantime, just get on with it.

2

LEADING TO WHERE?

Leadership is difficult but not complicated.

Leadership is the activity concerned with the navigation of a group of people from a defined starting point in the present to a different and simply defined state that exists in the future.

Step 1: Define your starting point. Keep it simple and be honest (even if it's painful).

Step 2: Define your end point. Don't be seduced into intellectual and complicated answers. But don't be afraid to be ambitious.

Leadership is the journey between these two points.

3

HOW TO GET THERE:
BEING DECISIVE

*Which is better? To take action and perhaps make
a fatal mistake – or to take no action and die
slowly anyway?*

Ahdaf Soueif, *The Map of Love*

NOW WE GET TO the meat of it. We've assessed where
we are and decided where we are going. Next, and most
importantly, we must consider the leader's defining task
– navigating their team along their journey between these
two points.

How are we going to get there?

It seems obvious, written down like this. It's just another
way of asking, 'What's our strategy?' – that's all strategy
is: a way of describing a journey from starting point A to
end objective B. And strategy is not as difficult as many
(often with vested interests) would have us believe. This,
however, is not a book on business strategy. This is a book
on leadership – and the leader's role on that journey.

By far the most challenging and important part of the leader's task lies not in strategy, but in execution. Put simply, strategy is explaining your route, execution is then getting on and actually doing it. As Peter Drucker, the father of business strategy, famously said, 'Ultimately all strategy devolves into work.' In other words, the role of the leader is to get stuff done.

Getting stuff done is really, really hard.

Let's talk about the business-changing, career-altering power of being able to get stuff done. For those who regularly visit the gym, it is like the compound lift of the business world, challenging your stamina, emotional intelligence, experience and wits. It's not part of the game, it is the game. It is the most unsexy and dull-sounding of all management tasks, but it is the *sine qua non* of the great leader. It is impossible to be a real leader if you can't get stuff done.

I was once asked by a very grand headhunter in her Mayfair office to describe my greatest strength. Being an emotionally repressed Northerner (before *Game of Thrones* made emotionally repressed Northerners interesting), I try to avoid answering questions like that, but put on the spot, I thought about it and replied, 'Getting stuff done.' There was an awkward silence, a clock ticked on the mantelpiece and she looked at me before writing a short unseen note on the pad before her. I said, 'You didn't like that answer very much, did you?' The meeting finished shortly afterwards. She never called back.

It may sound unexciting, but for a leader, there's nothing more exciting than results. And results require action.

The inability to get stuff done is where most leaders fail. This failure is the result of an accumulation of over-thinking and over-complexity when taking the steps we have outlined thus far: a simple, honest assessment of where we are today followed by a clear and easy-to-understand identification of where we would like to be at a defined point in the future.

This future should be ambitious; it should demand transformation and its benefit should be clear to all relevant stakeholders (for example: employees and customers). The actions to take between these points may seem terrifying, huge, unbridgeable and audacious, but they should not be that difficult to identify. Too often strategy is used as a means to obscure difficulty of execution, or as a panacea to demonstrate that the leader has delivered something clever for all to ruminate on. Too often it is seen as an end in itself. Strategy, by definition, is never an end; it is only ever a means to an end.

Ask yourself, how often have you created strategy documents (PowerPoint, anybody?) that have simply sat unactioned and forgotten on shelves? How often have you been the recipient of similar documents from others? How many sit on your desktop and in your email folders? These are the graveyards of most strategies.

Tell yourself you will never do this again.

The honest leader must first and foremost grasp the nettle: they must tell it how it is and define themselves by Churchill's favourite maxim: Action this day. (He liked it so much he had it made into stickers to save time writing it out by hand.)

The true leader uses strategy for one reason and one reason alone: to tell herself and the others around her what she and they must do to travel between point A and point B.

They then devote all their energies to execution.

Leadership is the journey between two points, and execution is everything

I work in advertising, and for many years I believed that our clients paid us to come up with ideas to solve their business problems. Many other businesses work on a similar principle (whether they like to admit it or not). One day, however, I realised I was wrong, that our clients didn't pay us for ideas, and that, in fact, ideas were easy. We all come up with ideas all the time. Ideas, it transpires, are ten-a-penny. The really, really difficult bit is the selection of a great idea and the turning of that idea into a concrete reality that, in our example, our clients were prepared to pay for and that would sell their product.

Ideas can only really be considered great once they have been executed. And executed excellently. Craft makes great ideas greater. I once worked with a very talented creative director. For one particular assignment he became obsessed with the idea that the solution was to project an advert onto the moon. Would this have been a fabulously effective solution for this brand? I can confidently say, yes, it would have been a fabulous solution. But the rather inconvenient fact that there was absolutely no way we could do it was a detail it took many months to get him to reluctantly concede. It therefore wasn't a great idea, it was a useless idea, and indeed simply got in the way of finding a great idea.

For example, have you ever thought of writing a book? I bet you have. You probably have a couple of ideas kicking around in your head right now. Have you ever got as far as writing anything down? Have you got to the point of persuading anybody to pay to read it? And, of course, there's books and there's *books*, there's films and there's *films*. The gap between these two states is the power of great execution. How many conversations did you have when *Big Brother* first took the world by storm in 2000 with people claiming to have had that very idea themselves? Or *Who Wants to Be a Millionaire?*. Yes, they might have had a similar idea, but they didn't actually *do* it, did they? Facebook was by no means the only social media start-up of its day. Some we vaguely remember (Myspace or Friends Reunited, anybody?), and many others died as soon as they were born. Why did Facebook succeed? Brilliant execution.

As I have moved through my career I have become more and more obsessed with the power of execution and craft. Everything that matters around us has had to move from a jumble of objectives, ideas and sketches, to a product or service that has ultimately risen above others (or that we choose over others). Even in areas where we perhaps feel we have no choice – for example, medicine. This transition is execution, and fantastic execution requires a strong will, steady nerves, a deep reservoir of self-belief and, ultimately, craft.

The leader takes ideas and executes them. Great leaders execute brilliantly. If you can execute brilliantly then you are a great leader. The rest of the leader's job is, if not easy, then certainly an awful lot *easier*.

Leadership is the art of getting stuff done

The majority of people in leadership positions spend much of their time prevaricating and actively avoiding action. It is why so many leaders fail.

I suspect that the very mundanity of this observation demands that I qualify what seems like a trivially obvious statement.

Just as nobody thinks they're a bad driver, no leader would admit to being unable to act. So, one more time – the single most important task of the leader is to get stuff done, and to encourage that behaviour in others.

As we have already established:

Leadership is the activity concerned with the navigation of a group from a defined starting point in the present to a different, clearly and simply defined state that exists in the future.

Often, this progress is difficult to see and feel – it is possible to lose an initially motivated and focused group because of inevitable difficulties along the way. These are moments of danger for the leader, and it's important at these points to temporarily take your own and your team's eyes off the top of the mountain ahead, which may, despite much effort, still look as far away as ever, and encourage everybody to look back and down to see how far you have come. If you're doing it right, you'll be amazed how high you can climb in a very short time – even if the end still feels a long way away.

The truth is that quick progress is only possible if you resolutely focus yourself and your team on getting stuff done. There are of course many other aspects of leadership, but without this, there is nothing.

It's one of those statements that seems so obvious you can feel a little short-changed by it. Surely there must be a whole lot more to leadership than this? Where's the mystique? I'm not too big on mystique. I'm here to help you get your team from point A to point B, and the only way that happens is if you start to get stuff done.

Leadership Impact (including a bit of maths)

One effective measure of a leader is Leadership Impact. Consider it like this:

Leadership Impact = (objectives + strategy + team + values + motivation) x (action)

In the above formula, the activities included in the left-hand set of brackets are those typically covered in books on leadership – and indeed are also covered at length here. Objectives, strategy, team, values, motivation – they're all important. The point of the equation however, is that without 'action', all these will achieve no forward movement. Or, put another way, lots of action and imperfect planning will make way, way more difference than the opposite. Take note and take heart. This is how we get started.

The leader should ensure a balance between activities to the left and right of the x, while remembering that *nothing to the left makes any difference without action*.

This is clearly anything but scientific (I did a degree in engineering, so am well qualified to comment), but it well illustrates the point: without action (i.e. action = 0), you can have all the strategy, clarity, team training sessions and spreadsheets you like, but your total net impact as a leader will be zero. Anything multiplied by zero is zero.

Viewed another way, you can be imperfect in many areas, but if you are decisive and focused on action, you will still create momentum and change. This is important for two reasons. First, it clearly lends a bias towards action in evaluating a leader and deciding how we will spend our time, and secondly, it should make us less paranoid about the precision of our planning and the inevitable weaknesses of ourselves and our teams. These shortcomings are diluted by the equation because it biases towards action.

What traditional leadership thinking has encouraged is the opposite. The consultants and workshops and PowerPoint presentations sit to the left of the equation. This is where too many leaders spend too much of their time and where the consultants and prevaricators thrive. It's possible to be very busy doing ostensibly useful things and never move from this bracket. What the leadership formula shows us is that though those things are important, without being paired with action they aren't just worth less, they are worthless: Leadership Impact = 0.

Creating action is the primary goal and daily task of the leader. If you create action you achieve Leadership Impact.

Given the unknowns of the real world, it is nearly always true that imperfect but intelligent progress is the best you can ever hope for – so take that as your primary aim.

The truth, in my opinion and observation, is that many leaders at all levels busy themselves with displacement activities, activities that are ostensibly important. It's just that these activities allow them to be doing things that appear to be important (things that most often fall into the left-hand side of our equation) to avoid the really scary and difficult bit: action.

Let's go back to our equation:

Leadership Impact = (objectives + strategy + team + values + motivation) x (action)

An overemphasis on the left and an avoidance of action is why many leaders fail. They fail not through lack of intellectual rigour or through lack of culture or talent. They fail because they spend too much of their time doing the things 'leadership convention' tells them they *ought* to be doing rather than doing the things they *should* be doing. They fail because their Leadership Impact is too low as a result of an underemphasis on action. They believe that leadership is about strategy, inspiration and vision, whereas in reality it's about impact.

If you're getting stuff done on your journey from A to B, you're leading. I'm going to explain how to do it better. Most of all, remember: leadership is the art of getting stuff done.

Taking decisions is taking control

When Lou Gerstner took the helm of IBM in the depths of its despair in 1993 he was widely lambasted by the business press for saying the last thing the company needed right then was a strategy. On closer inspection, what he actually said was not that they didn't need a strategy, but that they didn't need any more strategies – that the company's problem lay not in their ability to develop great strategies, but in their willingness to choose one and implement it. In other words, they needed to do less talking about it and more getting on with it. Gerstner stopped talking, started doing and famously reinvented Big Blue. And in his actions, rather than his words, lies a moral for us all.

Very few strategies or ideas are unique, yet many have the possibility of being enormously effective through smart, efficient and effective execution. Yet even the greatest strategy is nothing without the courage and ability to implement it.

Whole industries have sprung up to try and de-risk this process and to reassure leaders of the solidity of their thinking before they begin to execute. However, all the research studies in the world cannot remove the inevitable risks the leader must take for a project to be successful. Indeed, the search for the removal of risk more often than not leads to mediocrity.

How often do we find ourselves looking back on a project and feeling that it in some way fell short of its initial lofty ambitions? Was it the wrong strategy or did we lack the courage and skill to make that strategy a reality? Things only get tough when they get real. It's not possible to fail when writing a PowerPoint presentation (at least it's quite difficult to), yet as soon as you move to execution every step can feel like navigating a minefield. Here visible failure can feel only too close at hand. This is the all-too-real challenge of execution that many organisations and cultures do not do enough to understand and mitigate. It's easy to parrot the old cliché, 'It's okay to fail', but how often is that true? Great execution requires intelligence, teamwork, energy and perseverance. Most of all, however, it requires an effective decision-making culture which, as is always the case, must be led from the top.

Bringing strategy to life is about making decisions. Nobody who either is, or aspires to be, in a leadership position is going to admit that they are bad at this, but as every reader knows from their own personal experience, many are. To succeed as a leader you must ensure that effective decision-making is both your personal priority and baked into your cultural agenda, whether you run a corporate multinational or a Sunday league sports team.

The one thing nobody can help you with is which option to choose. For that you must rely on your and your team's intelligence, judgement and experience. What you can do is ensure you build a team that has a confident and capable decision-making culture.

Decide to decide

It seems kind of obvious, but this is the most important step. Tell yourself that through your actions you will ensure that decision-making is right at the top of your to-do list. Really – it can be that simple. Everybody takes decisions all the time, after all. The question is: are you focusing on the right ones? Are you getting the right balance between the important and the urgent, between thinking and doing? Are you seen to be decisive by those around you – effective teams must believe they have effective decision-makers leading them. Are you making sure that each decision is passed as far down the organisational structure as possible – more of an art than a science, but crucial to ensure an empowered, nimble culture.

There's a lot in that short paragraph, but you'll note there's nothing about being right or wrong. Despite the decision-making prevarication that often exists in organisations, rarely can outcomes be considered in terms of right and wrong – and people being annoyed, even lots of people being annoyed, is definitely not a reliable measure of whether you made the right call or not. Ultimately the only question should be: Did it take us closer to (or further away from) our goal? What I can say with certainty is the most wrong you can be is to not take decisions at all.

An elegant and simple tool both for structuring your own decision-making process and for encouraging a debate about that with your team is the Eisenhower Matrix, shown below.

Procrastination is the enemy of the decision-maker

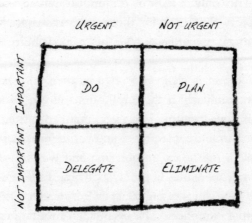

– and the procrastinator will typically spend their time on activities below the horizontal centre line, activities that in reality they should either be delegating or ignoring. The effective decision-maker and leader should make use of all four boxes, but the majority of their *time* should be spent above the line, doing and planning.

Decision-making is so often just taken for granted, but equally often it is done poorly, not thought about and not discussed. The key task for a leader is to ensure they and their team are aware that effective decision-making is an important part of the culture they want to create, and that it's firmly (and consciously) on their collective to-do list.

Stay true to Colin Powell's 40/70 rule

Only a foolish or irresponsible person would fail to agonise and fret over big and important decisions; leaders are aware not only of their own mortality, but also of the responsibility they bear for those in their teams. Most leaders, in my experience, feel this responsibility very keenly.

If a decision is clear and obvious then it's easy to implement; similarly if the implications of the decision are of no consequence. However, many decisions do have a measurable consequence and yet are not clear-cut. The problem that many responsible and well-informed leaders face, therefore, is paralysis in the face of what appear to be a series of big 50:50 calls. A leader's task is often further complicated by each side of the argument having well-intentioned advocates pressing its case (or more commonly the dangers of a misstep).

It's worth remembering here Colin Powell's 40/70 rule:

Don't take action if you have only enough information to give you a less than 40 per cent chance of being right, but if you have waited until you're more than 70 per cent certain then you have waited too long.

Don't act in haste, he says, but don't wait too long. However, this dictum can be read another way: that it is more desirable to act quickly and risk error than to wait too long and be wrong by default. Powell asks leaders to accept the possibility of error, but to get on with it anyway.

Decision-making must be reframed to include a fear of not making enough decisions quickly enough

This is ultimately the most liberating way to deal with decision-fear and to change your and your team's understanding of the decision-making process.

The leader should reframe their team's behaviour (and therefore culture) so that their 'fear' is based not on whether decisions are right or wrong, but rather on the far greater implications of not making decisions at all. A smart, execution-focused leader fears a lack of decision-making more than they do the fear of getting some of those decisions wrong. This can initially sound a little cavalier, but it is in my mind incontrovertible.

Firstly, any culture that prioritises fear of error over prompt action will ultimately become a slow, stodgy and dependent culture. Secondly, it is futile. Everybody and all teams get stuff wrong. Often, it is not even clear after the event that there ever was a 'right' or 'wrong' – just a series of different options, each one giving way to others. Acceptance that mistakes are inevitable and that uncertainty is a constant is the liberating place you want your team to get to. To steal a phrase, feel the fear and do it anyway.

And in truth – once you begin, it rapidly feels less scary. It just becomes normal. Nothing breeds a team's confidence like forward progress, and conversely, nothing destroys it like the inertia of slow indecisiveness. To quote a record company executive friend (after a post-work emergency pint or two) – there is nothing worse than a boss who cannot make a decision. He said it in a rather more post-watershed way, but we've all been there and felt his pain.

A leader's (and a team's) anxieties and inefficiencies around decision-making must be reframed from a fear of getting individual decisions wrong to a fear of making too few. This is achieved through the acceptance of the inevitability of error and a realisation that the worst mistake you can make is not making enough decisions quickly enough. This is a liberating place to be. It is of course helpful in the medium-term if more than 50 per cent are in your favour, but for sure crippling if they are too slow or too few.

Embrace the inevitability of error

Ultimately, like so much else in leadership, the answer to decision-making boils down to culture, which we'll come to in more detail in Chapter 4. A great culture is an environment where people are able to perform at their best. To be able to perform at their best they must be able to make frequent, rapid decisions, without undue or controlling fear of negative personal consequences. They must be not simply encouraged, but also expected to use their best judgement at all times within an effective support structure of peers and managers. The most significant markers in such a culture are not when all is well, but when things go wrong. This, as is so often the case, is the acid test of you as a leader. Can you stay true to the team's cultural principles when the shit hits the fan?

A wonderful example of using adversity to reinforce an effective decision-making culture comes from the aircraft carriers of the US navy. The flight deck of an aircraft carrier is probably the most complicated and valuable four acres of real estate in the world, as well as being one of the most tightly regulated and systematised. In this highly dangerous, high-performance world, team culture and behaviours rule supreme.

For safety reasons, every piece of equipment is numbered and must be signed for before it can be taken onto the flight deck. Even the smallest tool or part left behind and unaccounted for could lead not just to injury and death, but endanger the ship and therefore the fleet.

An engineer on one such carrier tells a story of misplacing a small item during a routine repair. After searching for hours he reluctantly reported the missing tool to his superior, and consequently the operations of the entire ship were forced to halt for twenty-four hours so that safety could be ensured – a hugely expensive and potentially dangerous state of affairs.

The engineer was convinced that he would be at best disciplined and at worst fired for such a basic blunder. The next morning, however, to his amazement, the captain, during his daily address to the ship, made a point of retelling this story, and praised him for his actions.

The moral of the tale is, I hope, obvious. The captain, as leader, recognised that maintenance of the culture of honesty and openness was what mattered most to the future performance and effectiveness of the fleet, not the engineer's error. If he had done otherwise he would have reduced the chances of the next mistake being reported, with all the consequent dangers that would bring.

This story also neatly reframes the old cliché, that it's OK to make mistakes. It is easy to interpret this phrase as promoting blasé behaviour – as though mistakes don't matter. In reality mistakes (as in this example) can matter very much. Rather it is about the creation of a culture that acknowledges the inevitability of mistakes; what matters is how quickly and effectively you and the team learn from and respond to those mistakes. In this example, the behaviour of both the captain and the engineer turned a potentially deadly mistake into a message that re-enforced and even strengthened their high-performance and high-trust culture.

We all get stuff wrong; it's how we as leaders respond that matters. The captain understood that culture is set ultimately by his behaviour, not by words written for presentations. Through praising the engineer's behaviour he made the ship more safe, not less.

Use checklists to prevent needless error and improve baseline performance

Pressure and stress do strange things to us. We've all been in situations where our brain just seems to seize up. We can't think straight and our actions slow. It happens to the best of us. Experience helps, but sometimes not much.

In his book *The Checklist Manifesto*, former surgeon

Atul Gawande proposes a solution that's a perfect fit for the No Bullshit Leader. He suggests writing lists – to be precise, checklists.

Gawande found that in a range of situations, from operating theatres and construction sites to cockpits and restaurant kitchens, creating clear checklists that carefully set out best practice very significantly improved outcomes – even if that simply meant a fluffier soufflé. Often these lists included what the practitioners would consider to be very routine information; in one high-end kitchen he found the instruction 'USE THE RECIPE' stuck to the wall. More seriously, however, in a global study he undertook with the World Health Organization he found that the introduction of simple pre- and post-surgery checklists led to a reduction in major surgical complications by 36 per cent and deaths by an astonishing 47 per cent. Importantly, the lists did not tell the team how to do their job, but rather reminded them of standard best practice. If they work in cases of life and death (never mind soufflés), they can help you.

Checklists have four key benefits:

1. They establish universal best practice in replicable situations – for example, the way in which you present a new idea to a client, the way a school department prepares lessons or how a sports team warms up for a training session to avoid injury. This frees the team to focus on the really difficult stuff, like the actual teaching.

2. They allow easy assimilation of new team members.

3. At stressful or high-pressure moments they reduce the number of decisions a team must make. Also, simply following the checklist can ensure that stress-induced foggy thinking doesn't get in the way.

4. They bring the team closer together through an agreed way of working. They can act as a kind of totem (see Chapter 4).

In addition, because they provide a universally agreed-upon baseline performance, they give everyone permission to speak up and be heard if they believe those standards are not being adhered to. This is particularly important in traditionally hierarchical environments such as operating theatres, but can apply everywhere.

The good news is that creating checklists is easy. In fact, in many cases Gawande found that the biggest hurdle was getting senior or well-established professionals to accept that checklists might be of use to them. In other words, getting past the egos.

Here's a checklist for creating a checklist:

1. The team should create it themselves.

2. It should be no more than nine items long. To return to the sports team example, you should be able to read and work through it in a huddle on the field right after the team have left the dressing room.

3. Wording should be simple, precise and fit on one page.

Checklists reduce the need for decision-making by 'auto-mating' replicable parts of your team's jobs. This has the dual benefit of raising baseline standards and freeing their minds to focus on the big stuff, where smart decision-making is crucial.

Effective meetings encourage effective decision-making

At the time of writing, that great entrepreneur of our age, Elon Musk, had recently spoken of the tyranny of 'middle management meetings'. He suggested that employees who saw no value in a meeting should simply walk out. Ask nearly anybody who works in an organisation of just about any type and they will recognise the problem: there are too many, they are too long, they start late, they overrun, they lack leadership and even apparent utility: what was that meeting for and what did we decide?

Though I sympathise with the problem, I'm not sure Musk's suggestion is a viable solution for most leaders in most organisations. Meetings are here to stay – and, in fact, a good, well-run meeting is a valuable and dare I say, enjoyable thing. The real solution is to make sure you have better-run, action-focused meetings. Make it a team rule (see Chapter 5). They also present key opportunities to build a decision-making culture.

Imagine if every meeting was a decision-focused meeting that adhered to a rigorously enforced cultural behaviour. It may be hard to imagine, but in practise it's not difficult to do. Effective leaders run effective meetings. This may sound obvious, but here's how:

Start on time

And insist all attendees are on time. Sloppy timekeeping suggests a sloppy culture.

Finish on time

It is only by exception that a meeting needs to last more than sixty minutes. Most humans have a maximum concentration time in one sitting of ninety minutes – if you have to have a meeting that lasts longer than this, make sure you schedule a break. Incidentally, most people can also only effectively concentrate for three ninety-minute intervals per day – so if you're organising a conference plan carefully and realistically. Those 8.30 a.m. to 6.00 p.m. days may look effective, but in reality they deliver diminishing returns, as the day goes on … and on.

Ensure there's a chairperson

At a business I ran we once decided to place a red chair in every meeting room to remind those using it that somebody should be in charge of every meeting. And everybody present would know who that person was. The chairperson sat in the red chair – and crucially, this very definitely was not always the most senior person in the room.

Set a clear objective

What is the meeting for? (Remember the learning objectives from primary school in Chapter 2: We Are Learning Today). I accept that sometimes it is necessary for large teams and organisations to have catch-up or status meetings. These can be very useful, indeed critical, but they still require clear organisation, objectives and actions. Don't allow 'weekly catch-ups' to simply sit, unmanaged and unloved in the diary.

Make decisions in the room

Ensure decisions are taken in the room. So often meetings are used to simply kick the can down the road. I have been in management teams where the same issue has been discussed at our leadership meetings week in, week out. Not only is this basic poor leadership, but worse than that, it is demoralising. There is nothing worse for a team to feel than that it is not in control of events. Taking decisions is taking control. Even decisions that are apparently unimportant, when taken promptly and acted on swiftly, can make a team feel invigorated and empowered. This is a very good habit to develop the team's 'decision-making muscle'.

Write it down

When you take decisions, write them down and circulate them with accompanying timings and actions. I believe that for most meetings minutes are a waste of energy and effort (as they are hardly ever read), but capturing actions is key.

Follow it up

Before you conclude, agree what happens next. If you've made decisions, then the 'next steps' should identify 'the who', 'the what' and 'the when' to ensure actions get taken.

The most wrong you can be is to not take enough decisions

Finally, let's consider how much is really at stake. Indecisiveness is an individual's reluctance to choose a path when presented with two or more options. Psychologists talk of loss aversion, which helps us better understand this phenomenon.

First described by Amos Tversky and Daniel Kahneman (the subject of a fabulous Michael Lewis book, *The Undoing Project*), loss aversion is people's tendency to prefer to avoid a loss than make a gain. In simple terms, people choose not losing a dollar over finding a dollar. Those paralysed by decision-fear often prevaricate to avoid a perceived loss, rather than act in order to gain.

Sometimes, the decisions we must make are huge. None of us will ever experience the terrible and unenviable pressures Eisenhower faced as head of Allied forces in Europe before he gave the final go-ahead to launch the D-Day invasion in June 1944. For us mere mortals, that was a scale of decision well beyond the more modest scope of this book and, I can safely say, beyond the experience of virtually every living human today. For the rest of us, how high are the stakes? Of course, they can sometimes seem quite high indeed, but we have to be honest with ourselves when we ask – just how high? Jeff Bezos talks about decisions being either one-way or two-way doors. The analogy is obvious. In practice, many of the decisions we take are two-way doors.

Let's be realistic. The biggest issue around decision-making is our natural hesitancy to make mistakes, to get it wrong. But getting stuff wrong isn't failing, it's just getting one decision wrong, and it's often not obvious what is wrong and what is right anyway.

Ultimately, very few decisions are irreversible, so live by the motto: *Try it. If it doesn't work, fix it.*

3

HOW TO GET THERE

Leadership is the art of getting stuff done.

⇩

Leadership Impact = (objectives + strategy + team
+ values + motivation) x (action). Nothing to the
left of the x makes any difference if action = 0.

⇩

Strategy is nothing without the courage to
implement it.

⇩

Stay true to Colin Powell's 40/70 rule:
Don't take action if you have only enough
information to give you a less than 40 per cent
chance of being right, but if you have waited until
you're more than 70 per cent certain then you
have waited too long.

⇩

Decision-making must be reframed from a fear of making mistakes to a fear of not making enough decisions quickly enough.

Embrace the inevitability of error.

Use checklists to protect your teams against needless errors and improve baseline performance.

Effective meetings encourage effective decision-making.

The most wrong you can be is to not take enough decisions.

4

CULTURE

Shall Rome stand under one man's awe?
Julius Caesar, Act 2, Scene 1

AS WE'VE ESTABLISHED, leadership is the navigation of a group of people from a defined starting point in the present to a different and simply defined state that exists in the future. And that it's difficult to do so. Why? Because leaders lead people and people, all of us, are complicated.

The leader's skill is to get the people she leads to outperform their competition – to achieve things that they would not otherwise have managed without her. Culture is the environment the leader creates in order for that to happen.

Culture is the most powerful and defining characteristic of most organisations, but often has little in common with the 'values' found on the website

In the lexicon of management-speak, few words are more abused than 'culture'. Perhaps it is no coincidence that activities related to the supposed creation of 'culture programmes' are among the most lucrative for the Leadership Industrial Complex that we met in Chapter 1. What company doesn't talk about culture on the front page of its website? How many companies use the same predictable adjectives? I contend, however, that for the majority of organisations the words used in the corporate brochure, or that are etched into the bronze artwork at headquarters, bear almost no relation to the actual real culture. Nor do they differentiate the organisation from thousands of others.

Virtually all organisations now feel the need to have a published set of values (a concept popularised by the book *Built to Last* by James Collins and Jerry Porras in the mid-1990s), from sports teams and schools to coffee shops and industrial giants. However, although each strives to differentiate themselves in many aspects of their performance (their product or branding, for example), there has developed a remarkable uniformity in their published values and, therefore by implication, their (claimed) culture. A study in 2015 by the corporate communications agency Maitland looked at the published corporate values of FTSE 100 companies and found that 'integrity', 'respect' and 'innovation' were claimed by fully one third of the companies. Imagine the money that has been spent, and will continue to be spent, on simply ending up with this homogeneity.

Of this group it seems that only Pearson, a publishing house, had chosen a set of distinct and individual values. Of its four, three were unique amongst this group:

'bravery', 'imagination' and 'decency'. Perhaps not coincidentally, these seem somehow both more thoughtful and more thought-provoking.

It is hard not to see the hand of the consultants with their 'propriety tools' in these findings. Nor, therefore, is it difficult to understand why so much cynicism now exists around the subject – a cynicism that in my experience stretches from the top to the bottom of organisations. That is because cynicism is proportionate to the gap that exists between what you claim and what you actually do; between our words and our actions. The smaller this gap – the less the cynicism, and of course, vice versa. It's true for people and it's true for teams.

For many organisations the creation of a set of values is a classic 'left of the x' activity (Chapter 3): it keeps many people busy for a long time and costs thousands (sometimes millions) of pounds – and often the consultants squeeze in again. Once agreed upon they are disseminated (often badly) and then, that's that. An organisation's claimed values are so often mostly meaningless wish lists because they are produced by committees and they rarely, if ever, come with actions attached. They are simply words the management likes or, more commonly, can agree on.

But culture does matter. The rise of 'values' as part of the corporate lexicon has done much harm through obscuring a proper and effective debate about culture within organisations. Values that are simply stuck on obscure effective discussion about what the organisation's real culture is. Nor do 'values' on their own define the kind of behaviours that make an effective team or culture. All teams have a culture, whether it be effective or ineffective, positive or toxic. The Maitland study did not measure the extent to which the actual culture was consistent with the claimed values. Now that would be a study worth reading.

It is worth remembering that Enron, whose leaders went to gaol and which went bankrupt from fraud, had its values proudly displayed in their lobby:

Integrity
Communication
Respect
Excellence

Culture is the behavioural environment the leader creates in order for her team to outperform – it's the ultimate super-weapon

For most teams and organisations, this is the reality. .

Cynicism around values exists because they are often generic and unrelated to the actual culture of the organisation – Enron's (as mentioned above) being an admittedly extreme example. A great and easy way to get a steer on the actual culture when you first join an organisation is to ask the person next to you: 'What do I have to do to get on round here?' Try it and see.

The answer to this question will inevitably (and sometimes uncomfortably) be a reflection of the behaviour of management. Of course, this isn't necessarily a bad thing; in fact, in a book about leadership, it's a good thing, as long as the behaviour of management is consistent with the best interests of the company, and the behaviours that the company has stated are those that matter most to it.

So, if the management team has integrity, is focused on relevant client-centric innovation and is consistently action focused *and* those are the things they have said are the key imperatives for the organisation, then all is good. The chances are that the culture will be coherent, mostly free of cynicism towards management and effective at delivering against the stated objectives.

Management behaviour is a far more powerful determinant of organisational culture than any number of training programmes, workshops and mission statements. In fact, I would go as far as to say that such is the ingrained cynicism toward mission statements and corporate values that they can get in the way of a good, functional and effective culture. The opposite is obviously also true – there is no point spending a ton of time and money defining your culture if management doesn't walk the walk.

Leaders lead people, and the complexities of leadership arise mostly because all of us are complicated. The leader's skill is to get the people she leads to outperform their competition – to achieve things that they would not otherwise have managed without her. Culture is the environment the leader creates in order for that to happen. That's it.

Studies have found that given time and budget, virtually every innovation can be copied, from a sales promotion (easy and quick) to a major product innovation (difficult and slow). However, organisational culture is to all intents and purposes impossible to copy. It is the most powerful and resilient of the weapons in the leader's armoury. It is all the more strange, therefore, that it is so misunderstood and, for many leaders, hardly consciously considered at all.

Effective leadership is so damn difficult because the leader must shape their own individual behaviour to create their stated desired culture. Culture is not something that the boardroom writes down and emails to the company. Rather culture begins and ends within the boardroom. Get it right there and the rest is a whole lot easier.

Parent–child (or 'dependent') cultures underperform

We have mostly grown up familiar with teams and organisations that work in a top-down, pyramidal way. The most important and highly paid people are at the top, and the most numerous, and often (although not always) the youngest and least well-paid are at the bottom, the widest part of the pyramid.

The problem with this model is that it tends to create a dependent culture: a top-down culture where those at the bottom are expected to wait for instructions from those above, and those above operate what is effectively a system of command and control. Those below become accustomed to looking towards the top of the pyramid for guidance and for the solution to problems, and those at the top become accustomed to passing instructions down. Even if this is not the stated desire of the organisation, this model actively disincentivises the majority of people to act and think for themselves. Our organisations have worked this way for many generations. We may have all stopped wearing bowler hats to work and knocked down (some of) the offices, but this culture remains.

Why does this matter? It matters because dependent cultures are less than the sum of their parts. When the real-world punches come, people don't know how to react, or do know how to react, but feel unable or unwilling to do so without instruction or approval from above. At best this is slow and ponderous; at worst it is useless. Our aim as modern No Bullshit Leaders is to create teams that are *greater* than the sum of their parts, cultures that take everyday mortals like you and me and create something fantastic. And it's not that hard to do. In fact, with a judicious application of cultural consistency and trust, I would contend that it's easier to build an empowered culture than a dependent one.

One of my favourite examples is the US retailer Nordstrom. Nordstrom is a US equivalent of John Lewis or Marks & Spencer, and like them it has built its reputation on its customer service. All new joiners are given the Nordstrom Rule Book. The book says the following:

Rule #1: Use your best judgement in all situations. There will be no additional rules.

Please feel free to ask your department manager, store manager or divisional manager any question at any time.

Although called a 'rule book' it is in fact better understood as a 'culture book'. It deliberately plays with our preconceptions of what a rule book is, and instead of defining traditional 'rules' for an employee, rather it defines behaviour and culture. And crucially not just for the new employee, but for the whole organisation. It tells everyone to use their best judgement, and it tells those with more experience that they cannot simply abdicate responsibility. The new joiner and the old hand are reminded of their roles and behaviours in perpetuating the Nordstrom customer-centric culture.

A UK shoe repair and key cutters, Timpson, took a similar approach. It's a large business comprising many small units tucked into high-traffic locations such as Tube stations, each unit isolated from its siblings and staffed by two to four people. By simply tearing up their internal command-and-control rule book and allowing each individual unit to act as entrepreneurial entities with shared objectives but individual strategies, Timpson liberated their culture and transformed their business. Their change wasn't rule driven, it was culture driven: a top-down, dependent culture replaced by a customer-first culture.

In his book *Adapt*, Tim Harford dedicates a chapter to the US army's bloody experiences in Iraq. In common perception, the military is the ultimate hierarchical culture, but this isn't true of all armies or all situations. In World War II for example, the German army is commonly considered to have outperformed all others (size for size), because of its culture of training its individual units to think and act independently while remaining clear and consistent with the overall objectives. Take for example the difference between:

A. We need to go and take that hill: let us tell you how.

and

B. We need to go and take that hill: you decide how best to do so.

In his book, Harford studies what General Petraeus found when he took over command of the US army in Iraq: a failing mission, a growing and bloody insurgency and a campaign that was deeply unpopular back in the US. The politicians wanted a solution, a way to win and/or a way out.

The army had become bogged down, and in trying to defeat the insurgency they had hundreds of small units dotted across the country based in small, isolated locations led by often relatively junior officers (in all armies the junior officers commonly end up carrying the greatest operational burden – sound familiar?). The army leadership gave very clear operational instructions to these officers, implicitly not trusting their judgement to act independently, believing in its top-down approach and that headquarters knew best. As their men continued to be lost, some officers stepped out of line and began to try and find their own solutions. However, Petraeus found an army that feared freedom of thought more than it valued the results this freedom sometimes created. Officers who didn't follow HQ's rules were disciplined or removed.

Petraeus inverted this model. He searched his command for those units who were the most successful and encouraged them to continue to refine their methods. Not only that, he created forums where their learnings could be shared unit to unit, so those who were succeeding could pass their knowledge along. Petraeus is remembered for his 'surge' in Iraq, but ultimately, Harford argues, he succeeded because he turned the US army from a dependent culture to a learning culture.

If Petraeus can do it with an army in a war zone, you can do it too.

In their own different ways, Nordstrom, Timpson and Petraeus inverted the conventional organisational pyramid. They did it by listening, by trusting and by changing from a policy of adherence to a centrally determined strategy, to a centrally determined culture and a locally determined strategy.

In each case they moved from before:

Leaders define both the objectives and the strategy, and act to preserve and defend their strategy even in the face of evidence that it is not delivering the desired results.

Result: The strategy becomes the objective.

to after:

Leaders define the objectives and the culture. Those on the front line (literally or metaphorically) define their own strategies by adapting to, and learning from, their successes and failures.

Result: The strategy is the culture.

A great culture is an effective culture, a culture that allows your team to outperform, and to outperform you must have teams that can learn and adapt to the real-world challenges they find all around them. A strategy that becomes a straitjacket will hold you back.

Many would agree that a rigid, top-down culture is the wrong way to run a modern company. It has become fashionable to talk about creativity or innovation, but like so much else, these are just words unless action is taken to make them part of the culture.

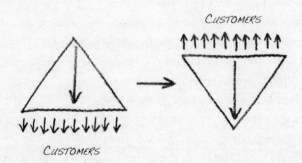

Leadership behaviour characterised by telling those below them what to do

Leadership behaviour characterised by asking 'how can I help?'

If we are to unlock your team's maximum potential and build a culture where everybody is focused on seeing and solving the challenges they face, then we need to turn the traditional organisational pyramid upside down. Or dispense with it altogether.

Traditional structures (represented by the left-hand diagram opposite) create dependent cultures, where highly motivated, well-educated and ambitious people are often discouraged from thinking and acting for themselves. The excuses used for maintaining such an inefficient way of working include governance, control and quality of outcomes, but I've long felt that if we don't trust the people who work for us then we should change them for people we do trust rather than imposing a slow, top-down, dead-hand approach that will hold you and them back. Many organisations talk a good game about people being their greatest asset, but unless they create a culture to enable their people to thrive it is just so much hot air. The simplified model on the right makes the people at the front line (client-facing staff, for example) the most important organisational figures. It transforms the leader into a mentor or coach.

A good example is the role (and cultural behaviour) of finance departments. Many companies behave as though they operate to serve the needs of the finance department – and the finance director is more than happy to subscribe to this view. In fact (with the exception of banks) finance is rarely the company's product; instead it's something that happens as a consequence of the company doing a good job of building its customer or client base. A culturally effective finance director asks the organisation, 'How can I help you to be more effective – you know what I need from you, but what do you and your teams need from me?' It's not difficult.

A leader must be able to attract great people *and* create a culture for them to thrive.

Create a decision-making culture. The key is a simple question: what do you recommend?

It may be breaking news to some leaders, but leadership really isn't just about them. It is about their whole team. An organisation that has only one leader and only one person making decisions is an organisation that will underperform. Managers of sports teams often talk about having leaders on the field. This isn't hyperbole, it's a recognition that pre-planning can only take a team so far. In the hectic reality of the day to day, a team must learn to function as a series of decentralised entities, often physically separate from each other. One measure of culture is how people behave when you're not in the room – which is most of the time. An effective culture therefore needs decision-makers everywhere.

In our fast-moving world, teams have to be prepared and able to tear up a plan when in pursuit of a clear and aligned objective. If not, then faster, more nimble competitors will race past.

The paradox is that the better you are at making decisions, the more your team may look to you (or indeed, you may expect that they come to you) to help them decide. If you're a small team this may sometimes be an effective way to work; if you're not, it will ultimately hold you back.

It is a well-observed fact that many entrepreneur-led companies stall once they achieve a certain size, and I am convinced a major reason is because the entrepreneur-founder(s) lack, or fail to develop, the skills to allow their team to function without their direct input. A less polite way of putting it is that they are control freaks who struggle to let go. The irony is that only by letting go can their baby grow to be an adult.

A former colleague recently approached me for advice. She had founded a small but very ambitious tech start-up with two colleagues. They were the techies, she the suit. Though the early signs for the business were good, she was finding working with her partners difficult. Though they were great at the technology, she found them terrible at taking responsibility. Weekly, if not daily, they would come to her and unload their concerns and worries onto her shoulders, asking for reassurance and support. Each of the three had their own clear roles and responsibilities within the team, and she had enough of her own problems without continually having to take on theirs as well. What, she asked, should she do?

Her problem will be familiar to many: it's the Friday afternoon meeting with a direct report who sidles up to your desk and unloads his concerns and worries onto your shoulders before leaving happily to the pub feeling a problem shared (for him at least) was a problem halved. You, however, head into the weekend carrying not just your problems but his as well.

I gave her the advice a former boss once gave me. I too had become used to taking on the concerns of others, and consequently becoming weighed down by theirs as well as my own. This made me less effective and more stressed, and reinforced a bad and culturally destructive habit. As my boss advised me, 'Don't allow people to pass the monkey from their back to yours. If they try, simply refuse to accept it.'

The key is to ask a simple question: 'What do you recommend?'

It's a powerful question, one that allows you to offer support and advice without allowing others to avoid taking responsibility. So useful is it that I have since met someone who had it pinned to the wall behind their desk, reminding all who approached that advice and support rather than monkey husbandry were on offer.

Claudio Ranieri

For example, let's consider top-level sport, the ultimate results-driven, high-performance environment. Membership of an elite team requires individual excellence as an entry-level requirement. The very, very best teams are an enviable blend of the greatest talent and the most powerful culture, making them, in their prime, all but invincible: Steve Waugh's Australians, or Pep Guardiola's Barcelona, perhaps. But what if, like virtually everyone else, you don't have a monopoly on the very best talent? Can great talent and average culture beat its inverse, average talent and amazing culture? An unfancied, unfashionable and relatively obscure English football team answered this question for the ages once and for all.

In 2016, Leicester City, under their manager Claudio Ranieri, defied near incredible odds (5,000:1 was widely quoted at the time) to win the world's most watched sports competition, the English Premier League, and in doing so achieved what is just about as close to the impossible as it gets in professional sport – outdoing even *Moneyball*'s famous Oakland A's.

Ranieri implicitly recognised that their only way to win was to create a culture powerful enough to outperform the superstar-studded teams against which they must compete every week. Brilliant leaders are not dictators but mentors. Technocrats micromanage; Ranieri built a culture, then focused on removing barriers (emotional or physical) to allow his team to perform at their best as often as possible.

He reportedly said, 'I will not speak of tactics'. Ranieri's strategy was his culture. Ninety minutes of football, like a business cycle, is a series of micro-strategies executed by those directly involved – those face-to-face with the challenge. Once the match kicks off, the manager is effectively out of the game; the team must be able to find their own on-field solutions. Ranieri trusted that his team had the knowledge and skills to deal with whatever on-field challenge they faced, and created a culture to enable and encourage them to do just that. He freed them to play without fear and so created a culture of on-field decision-making.

Nimbleness is the result of a culture that's good at making decisions

'Nimble' is one of those characteristics that organisations love to claim. Let's face it, in a world changing as fast as ours, what organisation wouldn't aspire to be fast on its feet? But what does it actually mean – how do you make an organisation nimble? What behaviours are required? My advice: every time you hear (or read) the word 'nimble' first tick it off on your business buzzword bingo spreadsheet that I presume, like me, you never travel without – and then mentally substitute it for 'a culture that's good at making decisions'. (I initially wrote: a decentralised decision-making culture, but though accurate, it sounded rather bullshit-y). It's a bit of a mouthful, but it's a phrase that's both more accurate and more useful because it describes the actual behaviour required. And of course it immediately explains why, although many claim it, very few achieve it.

No organisation that has a top-down culture can be nimble – it's as simple as that. So if you want to be nimble, don't spend time on process, spend time creating a culture of smart, responsible, decision-making at all layers of your organisation, from the boardroom to the receptionists. As with being pregnant, you can't be 'a bit' nimble.

'Ceasars' stifle your culture and limit your performance

Culture is the most powerful and defining characteristic of a team. It is the difference between your team outperforming and underperforming. The problem for a leader is not the lack of a culture (all teams have a culture) but rather to create the right culture, one that will allow your team to be on the winning side. In the majority of teams culture is thought to be an incidental thing that leaders pay little direct attention to or, worse, it is an unseen, but very strongly felt anchor that holds the team back. The challenge for the leader is that changing a broken, or even toxic, culture is tough, requiring strong nerves, a clear personal vision and plenty of stamina.

In a traditional advertising agency structure, the most powerful person is the creative director. You've seen *Mad Men* – Don Draper is a creative director: all-powerful, all-knowing. He sits on his white leather sofa in his corner office and is king of all he surveys. He is distant from the client and their worldly problems, but is a domineering figure in the agency. As a junior early in my career, I was told on day one that should I show an idea to a client before the creative director had approved it, I would be summarily dismissed. He is the feudal lord of the agency world.

When a client brief arrives at the door of an agency, via the client service teams, it winds its way upwards through the various layers of the business pyramid towards the creative director's corner office. It's slipped under the door, and then time passes. The great minds of the agency churn the problem over. More time passes. As if in a papal conclave, black smoke curls from the agency's chimneys. The client awaits an answer. Yet more time passes. More black smoke rises.

Then, eventually, white smoke. Celebrations! The creative director has chosen, a decision is made, and the idea, newly minted, beautifully packaged, wends its way back down to the client's door. The client, delighted (we hope) if a little frustrated at the weeks of black smoke and no news, inspects the idea. Why, they ask, does the agency think this is the right answer? And if the agency were honest, it would say, because Caesar says so.

It is a classic example of a top-down, dependent culture, one where only one person's opinion really counts, where, despite ostensibly being a creative organisation, originality is a threat to Caesar, his ego and his power.

Do you know a Caesar? Have you worked with one? Is there one in your organisation? Many companies have their Caesars, and Caesars, wherever they are, sitting in their literal (or metaphorical) corner offices, create dependent cultures. A dependent culture is one where, irrespective of the motivations and intelligence of the rest of the team, only one person's opinion counts. A culture with a Caesar cannot be an open culture; it is a culture where the aggregation of the talent in the company is less than the sum of its parts. It is slow and stagnant.

To become a nimble, networked, decision-making culture, you have to get rid of your Caesar(s) and with them the culture they create. It is time for your own Ides of March.

The purpose of culture in a modern and ambitious organisation or team is to liberate your people to outperform those of your competitors. Where a bad culture full of Caesars squashes talent, an effective culture allows the whole to be greater than the sum of its parts. There's no single answer to what your ideal culture might be, but the objective is to unlock the potential of everyone in your organisation.

I once went for an interview with a major, globally famous tech company. I was fascinated to meet them and hear them talk about the kind of people they were looking for and understand how they managed to maintain a high-performance culture in a company of that scale. I met the HR director. It was clear that she felt no need to be in sales mode, as they could pick and choose. We talked about culture and I explained my view: that a great culture allowed your stars to outperform, but that the real benefit came from the engagement and motivation of everybody, not just those the company considered to be its brightest and best. She asked what I would say if she told me that all 90,000 of their employees were stars? I told her that I wouldn't believe her.

Another job I failed to get.

But it's true. No organisation is packed with stars. Different people perform at different levels and, for a whole array of reasons, a person's performance varies over time. It's what makes us human. A great culture enables the combined efforts of its team's members to outperform the sum of their endeavours should they work at a competitor. Culture is not a nice, cuddly thing; it is a killer competitive advantage, and it has been proven to be the hardest innovation for your competitors to copy. They may be able to dismantle your latest smartphone and see how it works, but they can't pick apart and copy your culture.

Organisational culture is like concrete; to change it you must take highly impactful and physical actions

Peter Drucker famously said, 'Culture eats strategy for breakfast.' As a leader, therefore, a key skill is to understand how to influence and change it.

Culture is not a soft and squishy thing. It isn't providing free fruit in the mornings and yoga classes at lunchtime, or having enjoyable summer parties. Culture is a hard, physical thing that determines the team's ultimate performance: whether the organisation grows or shrinks, wins or loses, evolves or dies.

Imagine your culture being like concrete. Initially the concrete is wet. It is poured into a mould and can be manipulated, smoothed and shaped. You can squiggle your name into it, and the careless leave footprints. But over time the concrete sets. It's the same with culture.

To change a culture you must smash the concrete. Doing gentle, soft things will make no difference. Providing better perks doesn't fix a broken culture; you must do physical and visible things. And keep doing them. These actions should be clearly designed to smash the concrete, and must be seen and understood by all. Eventually, your new culture will also set, this time (if you do it right) into the shape you want.

The secret to smashing and resetting is to be clear why

you are doing what you're doing; it's not arbitrary:

1. Make clear what kind of culture the organisation must have and why.

2. List some of the behaviours (you don't need all the answers, remember – bias toward action) that you believe are important.

3. Take physical actions to signal that the old has gone and the new is here.

4. Ensure that this change visibly applies to you and your leadership team.

5. Hold your leadership team to account.

At this point, remember that irrespective of whatever mission statement or values you might carve into that expensively commissioned artwork in reception, ultimately, culture is the behaviour of management. To change your culture you must change the behaviour of your leaders, and if that's not possible, then you have to change the leaders. As I said, it's not soft and squishy.

This is how and why you remove the Caesars.

Leadership teams must be clear on desired behaviours, and must be prepared to hold each other to account. It's all too easy to berate those below; it is much more demanding to have difficult conversations with peers about whether they are being true to the behaviours they espouse.

In smashing the cultural concrete you must ask yourself, how do I make Monday feel different from the preceding Friday – for everyone? It is tempting here (as always with change) to think first of everybody else, but it is far more effective (and of course more demanding) to start with yourself. Although the concrete is difficult to break, some of the actions you can take are, on the face of it, simple, if not simplistic.

We are creatures of habit: we get up at the same time, choose the same meals from menus, say hello in the same way, put the same sock on first. If we weren't we couldn't get through the day – we can't agonise about every decision and action. Teams are the same; they acquire habits, behaviours, petty rivalries and private codes, mostly without even noticing. After all, none of these things affect the actual reality of what they are here to do. Do they?

On the face of it, these things seem trivial, but as a leader interested in change, you must jolt your team out of its comfortable patterns. You want them to see the familiar in a new way, and breaking their micro-habits is a fast way to signal change and force reappraisal.

So, for example: change the make-up of the team; change the criteria for who is in the team and who isn't; change where the team meets and how often; change the length of the meetings; meet in a light-filled, airy room; sit on sofas rather than round a table (or vice versa); change what the team is called; change the agenda. I could go on, but the point is to physically impact the team's culture through targeting its ingrained or unconscious habits.

If you run a sports team, make changes in the changing rooms, change the time you train, the duration and the content. Bring in somebody new (either as coach or player). No matter the kind of team, the approach works – signal change through, first of all, the breaking of the team's habits.

Now, of course, this is nothing more than the mise en scène, the creation of the context for change, but so much of change is this smashing of the concrete. And remember, change begins in the room that you, the leader, are in. It cannot begin outside if that room remains unchanged.

So break your team's concrete and you'll be amazed how the familiar can appear new. Try it and see.

Use the team's physical environment to help shape the culture you want

Few issues raise greater angst and debate than seating plans in organisations, and yet at the same time, few things are more visible manifestations of the culture. This is because many behaviours are hidden, yet how organisations choose to arrange their people is very, very visible. As such, use it to make your point.

Does everybody sit in offices?

If not everybody, who?

Does everybody have an assistant?

If not everybody, who?

Do people have their own desks?

Do you arrange yourselves in departments, and if so why, to what end?

Are there more and less popular spaces in the building?

How are those used?

I could go on.

Changing where people sit is a powerful blow of the hammer to the concrete. If you're doing it right, there will be howls of pain. Caesars love a seating plan in their favour.

Management books never talk about seating plans. Seating plans do not define cultures, but they do entrench them. Changing the plan doesn't set your new culture, but it is a very visible signal of change, of a smashing of the concrete. Some people will hate it, some will love it, everybody will notice.

When I took over as CEO of a failing advertising agency, one of the first actions we took was to pull down the offices, get rid of department boundaries and make everybody sit in client-centric teams. It was a visible change with a clear story of why, and it happened very, very quickly.

Did it alone transform the business? No.

Did Monday feel different from Friday for everybody? Yes.

Did it begin a process of change and crack the concrete? Yes.

It not about we, it's about I

Change doesn't happen in rooms full of clever people surrounded by empty pizza boxes. *Plans* for change happen in those rooms. Change happens when individuals begin to behave differently. Change happens as a result of action.

I have talked to many audiences about change, both as a leader of the business I run and in advising others. Contrary to popular belief, when you talk to an audience about change the reaction from many people is agreement rather than discomfort. Most smart people can see the challenges an organisation faces and welcome a leader with a clear plan to take the necessary actions; they can see the benefit to themselves. However, the actual process of change is frequently misunderstood; people think to themselves, 'Yes, I agree, *everybody else* does need to change, if only they'd all pull their socks up.' This is the opposite of the reaction you need in order to succeed.

What you need in order to achieve change is for every member of your audience to spend absolutely no time at all thinking about how others need to change and to think only of the change they themselves will make. The closer they are to the top of the organisation, the more this matters. Change happens when every individual grasps the need for them to change, and understands the benefit of that change. Change comes from many individuals doing small things differently – rather than, as is so often the case, from those same individuals being clear on what it is that everybody else needs to do better.

A short practical guide to determining useful values

I have expressed my scepticism at most of the activity and energy poured into trying to define a company's values. Not because values cannot be useful, but because often the creation of 'values' is seen as an end in itself, an HR-driven initiative that neither makes an impact on the organisation's effectiveness nor gets it closer to its stated objective.

Built to Last is a hugely influential book, however, like all tools, its principles are only as effective as the way in which they are used. Too often they are poorly employed or become a box to be ticked. In short, if you believe that defining or creating a set of values is an important exercise for your team, then read the book and do it properly – don't just rustle up a few adjectives you can all agree on and stick them on your website.

Most importantly of all, keep in mind what objectives you are trying to fulfil in choosing your values (and simple though it sounds, this is not a trivial question). If you're doing it to shape your culture, then values are worthless unless you accompany them with concrete and tangible actions to make their meaning real.

1. Start at the end

The point of values is to help define and shape your culture. Why? Because as we've established, an effective culture is the ultimate super-weapon, and near impossible to copy:

a) Write out in as few words as possible the culture you and your team believe you need to be successful.

b) Identify initial behaviours you need to share across the organisation in order to define this culture.

c) Finally – are there a small number of values that shorthand these behaviours?

2. Values aren't yours – they're everybody's

Culture may be best defined by the behaviour of management, but crucially, it doesn't *belong* to management. This is a critical distinction. An effective culture is one that belongs to everybody in your team or organisation. For this to be true the team must play a role in its creation, definition and maintenance. The 'open' culture we instituted at Grey London worked for us because the majority bought into and believed in its principles.

This wasn't by accident. We created a deliberate programme of activity – which we repeated and renewed at regular intervals, to ensure the involvement and engagement of people from across the business in its inception and definition.

This had three benefits: it improved our thinking, it ensured the culture was owned by the whole company, and it allowed full comprehension and engagement with this stage of the change process. It was time-consuming – but very effective. The consequences were that the culture was understood and owned by everybody: it's hard to be cynical when you did it yourself. The phrase 'That's not very open' became commonplace. Was it misused and annoying sometimes? Sure. Did the upsides outweigh the down? Undoubtedly.

3. Imagine the opposite

Most companies, as the Maitland study discovered, choose from a short, predictable and boring list of adjectives in order to attempt to define themselves.

One question I always ask myself is, for a given set of values, could I ever imagine wanting to be the opposite? For example, take what Maitland found to be the most common 'value': integrity. What organisation would ever claim not to have integrity, and therefore what benefit would be gained from using this word to define themselves?

I believe that in choosing a set of values it is important to ask, 'What do we gain by adopting these words?' and 'Are the words we have chosen the best way to achieve that end?' To return to integrity, what does choosing this word (above all others) tell your employees, customers and stakeholders? What does it tell them to do that they wouldn't do anyway? I would contend that in virtually all circumstances it tells people nothing new.

Instead of integrity, imagine if the company defined itself as 'A place where everybody is expected to speak up.' If integrity is a serious issue that the company needs to address, then what better way to ensure that happens than building a culture where those who try and bend the rules are held to account by their peers?

4. Say what you mean

Not only do many leaders choose from the same small pool of words in order to define their 'values', they also present them in the same way. The formula is: which four words are we going to choose to try and encapsulate who we are?

If this works for you – great. But remember, when doing this exercise, keep a laser focus on what you are trying to achieve: defining (or redefining) your culture. So if it is possible to simply encapsulate all that in a few short words, great. However, I believe that most often it is not. Perhaps the words can act as simple reminders of a broader definition (much as 'open' did for us), but if that is the case, don't forget about the broader definition.

Why not start with sentences, or even paragraphs? I get the benefit of brevity (although even with four words I wager that the majority of people, even in management, would be unable to remember their company's values), but I believe in this instance leaders should trade brevity for efficacy.

So, for example:

'Trust' might become: We believe that the team comes first. We trust in our teams and make sure we have each other's backs.

'Innovation' might become: We will continuously find ways to improve our service and delivery to our clients and customers.

Behaviours beat values

I believe a more practical and tangible approach – either as a stand-alone or to accompany values – is to consider 'behaviours'. If culture is about how we behave, then defining cultural behaviours would be a smart place to start.

When asked this in my last CEO role, I would answer that, 'Our strategy is our culture.' We had a name for it: open. The idea wasn't unique, but it was a simple, memorable and effective summary of the behaviours we believed would create and sustain an effective culture:

Our objective: to be the best.

Our strategy: to create a superbly effective culture that allows our talent to outperform that of our competitors.

Our culture: open.

Being original, unique or clever didn't feature. It was simply about what would get us to our goal.

What was interesting about 'open' is that it was never a 'value', but rather a shorthand for our culture and therefore for a way of behaving, a way of behaving that we talked about with both our clients and employees and with whom it resonated equally well. It consistently passed the crucial test of 100 per cent employee awareness, and I'm sure it still does.

Importantly, 'open' was accompanied by behaviours that gave it both credibility and meaning.

So, for example:

1. No one of us is as smart as all of us. We held workshops (that we ran) with everybody in the organisation to ensure we both explained our

cultural vision and got everybody to help us shape and improve it. Culture may be best defined as the behaviour of management, but to be successful it must belong to, and be understood by, everybody.

2. We are our most important client. We all had to be prepared to dedicate time to fixing our own challenges, because only by doing so could we become better at helping to fix the challenges of our clients.

3. Kill the processes. We tore up all our defined processes and allowed client teams to define their own client-centric solutions (in the same way that Timpson did, see page 61).

4. Removed departments. We encouraged greater client-centricity by mixing everybody up across the organisation. You couldn't tell what job people did based on where they sat, but you could tell what client they were primarily responsible for. We put our clients' needs ahead of our own structure and egos.

5. No templates. We got rid of set strategic templates to make our strategists think from first principles rather than in familiar boxes.

6. Management as mentors. We reframed our leaders as mentors to projects, rather than insisting that work be 'signed off' by them before it went to clients.

This is by no means an exhaustive list – and in fact was a list only ever written down after the event. Rather, these and other behaviours were a continuous stream of initiatives intended to explore and push the boundaries of 'open' and determine, in a pseudo-Darwinian way, what version of it would work best for us.

In fact, I have deliberately included in the list above some things that didn't work. For example, No. 5, the tearing-up of templates, was a disaster. Without a template of some description we ended up with anarchy: nobody knew what they were supposed to be doing. Within two weeks they were hurriedly reinstated. Does that mean this approach doesn't ever work? Of course not. It just didn't work for us, with the culture we had and the talents we employed at that point in time. Would I be prepared to do this again in different circumstances? Absolutely. Likewise, would all of those that worked for us work for everybody? I am sure not.

Other parts of the list caused problems, but were less black and white. For example, removing department boundaries was for many people deeply unpopular, as was pulling down all the offices. The finance director finding himself sitting next to two rowdy Scandinavian art directors was fun for both (and everybody else) for about half a day – and then quickly became a total pain for all concerned.

So version 2.0 was an organisation where you still couldn't tell who did what by where they sat (including the finance director) and without clear departments, but we performed a little 'social engineering' to ensure we minimised painful clashes such as this. The environment remained true to the principles of the cultural 'story' and set the cultural behaviours – while still working for everybody. Ultimately, the benefits of the change outweighed the new challenges it threw up – and when it didn't we tried something else.

Totems can be a powerful shorthand for your culture

Sir Clive Woodward is one of the most celebrated sports coaches in England and perhaps the world. In 2003 he famously led England to victory in the Rugby World Cup in Australia, beating the hosts in the final with virtually the final play of the game. He then took on an arguably greater and even more complicated challenge and became Director of Sport for Great Britain during the London 2012 Olympic Games, leading the team to a record medal haul.

Immediately on taking the Olympics role, Sir Clive recognised the critical importance of building a culture that linked hundreds of competitors, their coaches and support teams. Like all cultures, this wasn't a soft, squishy, feel-good affair, but was about creating an environment where the whole became greater than the sum of its parts. It was about winning on the most visible, global stage there is.

In talking to the coaches and athletes, Sir Clive recognised that his first challenge was to persuade the disparate sports that there was actually a benefit to each of them, from the most lowly to the most famous, of a shared culture. He did this through focusing on the commonalities – the things they shared.

A critical common factor was identified very early on, that of health and hygiene. The teams would be crammed together in the Olympic Village for several weeks, and the transmission of even one minor cold could derail the dreams of dozens of athletes, if not the whole team. However, despite its importance, it quickly became apparent that individual sports had very different standards and procedures, which in the past had led to almost open conflict between them, as managers attempted to keep their athletes healthy.

The first step was to agree standard procedures across Team GB for the maintenance of a germ-free environment within the team's Olympic Village. This covered everything from the rules governing the isolation of individuals who were suspected of being ill, through to the cleaning and sterilising of drinking bottles. The rules weren't agreed top-down, but bottom-up by the athletes themselves. Ideas and suggestions for improvements were circulated and ultimately approved and implemented by the whole team. It was the perfect alignment of a shared objective – staying healthy – with a shared culture. Clearly identified behaviours made that culture real.

One idea, however, took on a special significance. The team installed at every doorway (internal and external) in the Team GB Village an antibacterial handwash dispenser. The behaviour the entire team agreed to was that nobody, no matter who they were, no matter how important their journey, no matter how late, could pass through a doorway without first washing their hands. Often this entailed an individual washing their hands a dozen times to pass from one side of the camp to the other. It led to queues (to be fair, the British love a queue) next to open doors as athletes, PRs and coaches waited to wash their hands before passing through. The team self-policed the rule and woe betide anyone who tried to sneak through without observing the ritual. The most junior members could (and would) admonish the most senior if they were spotted sneaking through without washing.

The effect of this culture (because remember, culture is about outcomes) was that there was not even a cough or sniffle in Team GB for the duration of the Games, allowing all athletes the best possible chance of performing at the top of their game when it mattered most. And ultimately, of course, leading to a record medal haul.

However, the handwashing is interesting for us as it took on a greater significance than simply hygiene. It became a totem for the togetherness, single-mindedness and attention to detail of the whole team: a group who had mostly never met before the Games and would never all be in the same place again once it was over. It became their 'thing' for the duration. It wasn't Sir Clive's thing; it belonged to the team and was policed by the team. There were no Caesars.

The hand sanitizer became a daily (often hourly) physical reminder, a totem, of the entirety of the values, behaviours and culture of the team: it was theirs and only theirs. If outsiders found it a little obsessive and weird, all the better. It reminded Team GB of the bonds that linked a group of people who had nothing in common, other than the experience of those two weeks, yet they shared a universally understood culture that led to unprecedented success. Did a few thousand pounds worth of hand sanitizer make the team the most successful British Olympic team ever? Probably not. Did it play a significant part? Without doubt, yes.

Totems are powerful, in my opinion many times more powerful than the values that so many shout about on their websites. Totems are tangible signifiers of a wider culture. They can be anything, but they must belong to everybody. When seen or used they are reminders of what the team has in common and what makes them different. At Grey, it was our seating plan – weird, I know. As new people joined we watched their discomfort, their lack of an office, their lack of a department, of clear structure, the apparent lack of rules. But then it clicked; they got it, they became part of it and then they too sat back and watched the next new arrival. Of course, sometimes people never got it and left, but for those who did and remained, that made the bond stronger still. It built our sense of otherness and difference. We wanted to stand apart, be iconoclastic and different.

Totems matter. What's yours?

Culture is the behaviour of management: if you don't walk the walk, it's all just bullshit

I believe that culture is the most powerful and defining characteristic of most organisations. A very small minority may have uniqueness of product or talent for which this may not be true, but for the rest of us mortals, it undoubtedly is.

I have heard leaders say that culture is something they cannot influence. Nothing could be further from the truth. The leader is the single most important cultural influence, bar none – whether they realise it or not. Ultimately culture is the behaviour of management – no amount of values and mission statements will change that fact.

Leaders lead people, and that's where it gets complicated, because people are complicated. The leader's skill is to get the people she leads to outperform those around them – to achieve things that they would not otherwise have managed. Culture is the environment the leader creates to enable her team to win. That's it.

4

CULTURE

Culture is the most powerful and defining
characteristic of most organisations, but it often has
little in common with the 'values' found on
the website.

⇩

Culture is the environment the leader creates in
order for her team to outperform. It's the ultimate
super-weapon and nearly impossible to copy.

⇩

A parent–child culture will underperform, as it
disincentivises people to use their best judgement or
think for themselves.

⇩

Create a decision-making culture. The key is a
simple question: what do you recommend?

⇩

'Nimbleness' is the result of a culture that's good at
making decisions.

⇩

'Ceasars' create ineffective cultures and lead to underperformance.

⇩

Organisational culture is like concrete; to change it you have to take highly impactful and physical actions.

⇩

Use the team's physical environment to help shape the culture you want.

⇩

Most exercises to determine 'values' are a waste of time. Defining behaviours is more effective and useful.

⇩

Totems can be a powerful shorthand for your culture.

⇩

Culture is the behaviour of management: if you don't walk the walk it's all just bullshit.

5

BEING FOLLOWED

Finding, keeping and inspiring your people

*The first method for estimating the intelligence of a
ruler is to look at the men he has around him.*

Niccolò Machiavelli

THUS FAR, WE HAVE considered the key stages of the
leader's journey: how to understand and define its start,
its ultimate destination and the central role the leader
plays in establishing an effective culture. But a leader
must also have the right people in her team. She must
retain, hire, motivate, coach and cajole to ensure she
jealously acquires the best and most talented people she
possibly can. Along with building an effective culture
she has no more important task than this. Whatever your
style, all leadership ultimately boils down to one simple
truth: leaders need followers.

A leader, to be effective, must improve (or at a
minimum maintain) the performance of a group of people
against a clear set of measures. No matter what your task,
whether a team leader on a production line, a firefighter
or a tech entrepreneur, ultimately your success as a leader

is dependent on your ability to positively influence the behaviour of those for whom you are responsible. Sometimes, for the fortunate, this takes place in a benign environment; for others it can be very hostile. It may even seem initially for some that your greatest battle is with your own team rather than the competition. The context has limitless variations, but the leadership question remains the same: can you mould a group of individuals into a team and convince them to follow you?

Most organisations are just buildings full of people. What makes one better than the other? Talent and culture

To my shame, it wasn't until I had become a CEO myself that I realised I hadn't actually spent that much time thinking about what it was that made one business in my industry better than another. Of course, I could recognise which were good and which were bad, that was easy, but what was it that made them this way? (And at this stage we were very clearly one of the bad ones.)

What was it that made one company a mile down the road so much better than ours? After all, I reasoned, there was no outwardly obvious difference between the two. It's true of all teams. Sure some teams are chock-full of superstars, but most aren't. Nevertheless, it's possible to look around you and see some teams that clearly outperform others. It's obvious, but I hadn't really wondered why. Of course it's down to leadership, but what does the leader actually do to create this state of affairs?

Many businesses and organisations, I reasoned, be they accounting firms, management consultants, sports teams, banks or in the service sector, are simply buildings full of people (and they don't even own the building). Furthermore, over time competitors will share a large amount of the same employees between them as individuals move from job to job, role to role.

So to reframe the question, how was it that someone else's building with people in it was so much better than ours? Or, if yours is one of the good ones, why is it that your building full of people is outperforming the others?

'Buildings full of people' is a frustrating, but at the same time, liberating concept. I puzzled over this for quite some time, searching for a clever or sophisticated answer.

Ultimately, I discovered no sophisticated answer. The only answer I found led back to our old friends culture and talent. We've already talked a lot about the transformative effects of culture, and its power is such that different cultures can make the same person appear either a rock star or a failure. It's important to get it right.

The other factor is talent. Striving to create a great culture is futile unless the leader is also able to identify, attract and retain great people.

We're all in the talent acquisition industry

In a business context, the CEO is responsible for the performance of the business, sets the culture and ensures that the people are right for that business. If that's all you do – you're not going far wrong. But you don't have to be a big-shot CEO to have talent acquisition at the top of your to-do list. In fact, for many leaders it can be one of the few things over which they have a high degree of influence and control. Take a Sunday league football coach for example – why would local kids choose you? How do you keep training interesting and varied enough to make sure they keep turning up when its windy, cold and wet (and don't simply switch on the PlayStation instead). The majority of leaders lead within the context of a wider organisation (a head of department in a school, for example). These leaders will have their own objectives, and their ability to attract and retain the very best people into their team will be key to them succeeding. In many organisations people are also relatively free to move around between teams, and I see time and again how some leaders outperform simply because they create an environment that people want to be part of, and so choose them rather than one of their peers.

As we covered at length in the previous chapter, for the ambitious and successful leader, creating a culture that attracts and retains the best people is not just something that is 'nice to have' once all the serious stuff is taken care of. Rather, it is the surest way for that leader to achieve their own personal goals. Every leader should follow the same three principles: focus on the core objective; build the right culture; retain and hire (or select or attract) the best possible people.

For this reason I am against the proliferation of job titles such as Chief Environment Officer, Chief Culture Officer (I even once saw Chief Happiness Officer ...),

Chief Talent Officer and the like. Look, I get it. Human Resources is not exactly a culture-friendly term, but the CEO cannot outsource culture, growth or talent. These aren't just three of the things she needs to worry about, amongst hundreds of other things. These are *the* three things. I once asked a CEO if he knew who his twenty most important people were. He looked at me, frustrated, and said he had been asking HR for the information for months. He'd outsourced the knowledge.

Leaders need teams, but ultimately they cannot suggest to the organisation that the retention and attraction of the best talent is the role of a department. It isn't. It is the primary goal of the organisation, and therefore must be a primary task for the leader(s). This principle doesn't just apply to CEOs of course, but to all leaders, whatever the size of their team or their position in the organisation. All team leaders must jealously seek to acquire and retain the best people and to take responsibility for doing so. It doesn't mean you'll always get your way, nor ensure you always make the right calls, but you can't build a strong team any other way.

In a world as complicated as ours, a world of such rapid change and fluidity of people and finance, securing the best people and fitting them into the most effective culture is a leader's primary task. I would go as far as to suggest that for many companies it is useful for them to consider themselves as being in the talent acquisition and retention industry – rather than in the customer acquisition and retention industry.

Another way of making the same point is that a great

culture alone might make a good team, but without a great culture *and* great talent you won't ever be the very best. Obvious, no bullshit, stuff. Get the right people and the right culture, both of which are focused on your objective, and the results will come.

The obvious, but as it transpires very difficult, question is: what does a culture that attracts and retains the best people look and feel like? How must the leader behave? I struggled for many years to find a clear and practical approach for myself and the leaders around me – one that would work for everybody. Eventually, the answer I hit upon was to ask of myself and them this one simple question:

How good are you for the careers of those who work for you?

It's a bit of a mouthful, but just chew it over for a moment: it's powerful. It's a great question to ask yourself and a great question to ask of others. Obviously here I've framed it in the context of a business, but it can easily be adjusted for any leadership environment.

Of course, it isn't diagnostic; the leader must do more than simply ask this question if he seeks to improve and nurture the performance of his team. But it's right on the money if a key aspect of your strategy is talent acquisition and retention: which it should be.

The answer is, of course, that we want our leaders to be great for our careers – our 'career' in this context being the aspect of our personal ambition that is synchronous with that of the team. If your team thinks you're great news for their own personal ambition (whatever that might be), then that is the surest way to keep them motivated, growing, thriving and striving. We want that for those who work for us and we want that for ourselves. 'Liking' has little to do with it, you'll note.

The opposite also makes the point. Ultimately, if we aren't good for our teams' careers we will fail not just to retain our best people, but against our final objective.

The question asks us both how well we are doing against our team objectives and against the individual ambitions of our team members. Aligning and succeeding against both is as close to leadership perfection as I can imagine – the more you fall short as a leader against one or both, the greater the lag you will experience in achieving your own personal ambition.

There's a lot more to managing people than this, but if you only ask yourself and those around you one question, this is the question to ask. Because imagine how great all our teams would be if the answer to it was always a resounding, 'Fantastic'.

A great team is comprised of great individuals who see the fulfilment of the team's objectives as wholly aligned with the fulfilment of their own ambitions

Mike Brearley is one of the most successful (and most enigmatic) of England cricket captains. To the uninitiated cricket is a baffling sport, yet its adherents obsess over its endless variations and layers of complexity. It is almost unique in that it is a team sport played out through a series of deeply personal and individual duels. A trained psychoanalyst, Brearley has throughout his life studied, from both the inside and the outside, the construction and leadership of successful cricket teams and, more widely, teams of all types.

'One could almost say,' states Brearley in his book *On Form*, 'a [successful] team is an individual. Each team has its own character, style, demeanour … It has its characteristic weaknesses or vulnerabilities, as well as strengths … The team is an individual greater than the sum of its parts. Similarly, the individual is a team, with many of the qualities of teams, a composite.'

Just as Newton showed that white light is a combination of a spectrum of colours, Brearley encourages us to consider the members of our teams (and indeed ourselves) as a mix of individual elements: strengths, interests, weaknesses, prejudices, beliefs and desires. We too appear to be a homogeneous whole, but are in effect a blend. As when white light is filtered through a prism different colours become visible, so we – at different times, in different situations and in different cultures – behave and think differently. In this way, an effective leader creates a culture that rewards (emotionally and physically) the behaviours, beliefs and actions that most effectively help the team achieve their goal.

Elsewhere in the book, he quotes the psychiatrist Pierre Turquet (a former Olympic fencer) writing on why teams succeed or fail. Turquet calls selfish members 'singletons' and compliant members 'membership individuals'. The singleton sacrifices the team in favour of their own desires or glory; the 'membership individual' sacrifices themselves to the team leading to 'dull unanimity'.

These two extremes are familiar to us all. Few argue for dull unanimity, but many leaders struggle with the challenges of maintaining a coherent team and culture that can allow individuality and nonconformism.

Turquet has a third category of team member, the 'individual member', one who keeps their individuality and style while playing their role and contributing fully to the objectives and direction of the team.

To quote Brearley again,

> We must [each] fight our own corner, develop ourselves, be selfish … But if we are only that we are limited and stunted. We need also to be unselfish, to want the best for bigger groups than our little selves … At times we have to constrain ourselves in the interests of the team; no one can do exactly as he wishes … By being in a team, we also, potentially at least, have the benefit of the team's support, especially when things are hard individually. Teams succeed when there is a happy balance between looking after the self and looking after the team.

Just as when we consider our team's objectives and we strive to ensure balance between the benefits to the individual and the collective, so we should strive for balance in the creation of our teams. A team is comprised of individuals who each bring with them their own desires, insecurities, passions and fears. A successful team allows each, at different times, to pursue their own ambitions within the parameters of the objectives of the team, while at other times the needs of the whole (or of others) come first. Thus, in a successful team, sometimes we lead from the front, and at other times from the back. Each of us must and will at different times contribute to, and draw down from, the collective energy and resources of the whole. The leader's role is to ensure that her team members find and collectively maintain this balance.

In most situations, the people around you have choices; you, as the leader, should strive to ensure that this is the case for your team. In simple binary terms, individuals should have the choice to stay or go. The counter-intuitive implications of this are that a great leader should create as fluid an environment as possible. The leader's job is not to make the best of a bad job, but to create an environment so good that nobody ever wants to leave. This is the fallacy of many modern employment contracts; if people feel trapped by their contract, then they will never be full, high-performing members of the team, and thus it is self-defeating, damaging not just them but the performance of the whole.

A great leader should strive to create an environment that their people actively choose to be part of, and for that to be true, the corollary must be that they have the option to leave. As the leader it is easy to fall into the trap of seeing the world only in terms of what is in your interests, so you must continually remain aware of what is in the interests of those who work for you.

A great example can be found at Saracens rugby club. Saracens are among Europe's most successful rugby teams – one of only four clubs to have won the sport's highest prize, the European Cup, back to back. The club recongises that the working life of a rugby player can be, to misuse Thomas Hobbes, 'violent, brutish and short'. Even the most successful careers come to end – and then what? Saracens' players are encouraged to develop interests beyond the sport, and are given every Wednesday off to further their educational or business pursuits, helping them acquire experience and knowledge that bridges to a life beyond rugby, even while that remains some years into the future. To date, players have founded a coffee roasting company, a brewery, restaurants, consultancies and a media business, amongst others. As former Saracens CEO Edward Griffiths told the *Guardian*, 'We had a simple principle that you treat people unbelievably well and in return they will try unbelievably hard.'

The best leaders ensure a continual confluence of the needs of the individual and the needs of the collective. A great team is comprised of great individuals who see the fulfilment of the team's objective as wholly compatible with the fulfilment of their own ambitions.

Always remember: there are lots of 'I's in 'team'.

Great teams need their stolid professionals and maverick playmakers – and a culture that values both equally

In Chapter 4 we met Caesar; to him all nonconformity was a threat. We've learnt that our organisations aren't machines, and far from being a threat, in a networked organisation (full of millennials used to living in a very networked world) we need to actively seek out those who Niall Ferguson refers to in his book *The Square and the Tower* as 'freaks and misfits', people who challenge orthodoxy, people who themselves are prepared to lead.

In a way, this is one of the greatest challenges for a modern leader, balancing the widely acknowledged need to accommodate nonconformists, with the reality of doing so. The truth is that homogeneous teams are easier to run; however, the problem is they just aren't as effective.

The great leader keeps her eye on the prize. We don't want to manage to the middle; we want to be the best. To be the best we need radical, not just evolutionary solutions, and those solutions will come more readily from diverse teams comprised of eclectic members.

The creation of such teams is a challenge. It's easy to hire mavericks, but it's difficult to meld those mavericks into a team – that's why leadership is difficult. A leader must consider carefully the needs of the whole team and the role each member must play. Some must be square pegs in square holes: reliable and predictable. Others must be misfits, free to roam and challenge. Take the example of a football team. A successful team needs its safe, reliable defenders who play within a structured game plan, and it also needs its maverick playmakers. The defenders must deliver a predictable ninety minutes of dependable reliability, whereas for the team's *libero* nothing may go right for eighty-nine minutes, but with a single moment of inspiration he wins the game. To succeed the team needs, and must value, both, and the defenders cannot feel like second-class citizens. The trick is to find a balance, which, as with all great teams, allows the whole to be greater than the sum of its parts.

Diverse teams win

To quote one piece of evidence among many, a 2015 McKinsey report on 366 public companies found that those in the top quartile for ethnic and racial diversity in management were 35 per cent more likely to have financial returns above their industry mean. I see the evidence every day. I see it where we do have diverse teams and I see it where we don't. Diverse teams outperform those that aren't.

By diverse, I mean in every sense: gender, ethnicity, social background, physical ability, sexuality and so on. There are many reasons why building diverse teams and companies is the right thing to do. It's right for our organisations and it's right for our society. And, crucially for this book, it's better for you as a leader.

Nobody gets this right all the time. I experience daily how difficult it is. But this is just another example of the leader's challenge; we are always halfway up the mountain. The important thing is to be striving to improve: to be doing stuff.

The best way to tackle this difficult issue is to accept and actively promote the fact that diversity in an organisation isn't desirable only to those who are currently under-represented – it is desirable for all those who have the organisation's best interests at heart. (This hopefully should include everyone in your team; if not, switch them out fast.) This makes the search for greater diversity a critical task: if we get it right we outperform, and outperforming is why we're here.

Understanding this fact is the fastest route to solving the knotty problem of diverse hiring. I'm often challenged with the argument that, yes, diversity is an undoubtedly desirable outcome, but when considering any individual hire or promotion, you have a duty, even a moral responsibility, to hire the best possible person for the role, irrespective of who they are. This is often used as an argument for status quo hires – an argument that leads to less diverse teams.

Of course it's true, nobody wants to feel they have been given a job or a promotion because of their colour or gender, but the answer is to consider the team rather than the individual as the basic and most fundamental building block of the organisation, just as a complete atom, rather than its constituent parts, should be considered the basic building block of matter. In this way, you consider every individual no matter their background, skills, gender, temperament or any other factor, in the context of *the needs of the team*. This way the best candidate is the candidate that helps build the best team. And the best teams are diverse teams.

A leader must also take care that a well-intentioned desire to increase diversity does not have the unintended (and unwelcome) side effect of creating division. The leader's intention is absolutely not to segregate their team. For this reason she must always be focused not just on diversity, but its twin – inclusion. In fact, you could consider the creation of a truly inclusive culture that works hard to level the playing field for all, to be the truest way to create a diverse team of people.

Ensure equality of opportunity

A leader must understand that some 'accepted' aspects of how organisations are traditionally run (the idea of a fixed working day, for example) make life very difficult for some people, and that's bad news for the overall effectiveness of the team. A typical example involves childcare. It remains the case that childcare responsibilities in most families fall more on women than men (and not just when children are babies). These are large-scale societal issues, but leaders can focus on these and find both structural and cultural solutions to allow people (both men and women) to work effectively and still be great parents. This is a huge topic, and there is not the space here to begin to do it justice, but it would be remiss for a 'healthy leader' (more on that in Chapter 7) not to focus hard on this type of question. Not just because it's the right thing to do, but crucially because it will lead to a better, more effective culture where more of your best and brightest are able to perform at their peak more of the time. And they can do that because you are enabling the different aspects of their life to cohabit rather than compete.

Leaders striving to build a healthy working and cultural environment should focus on three key questions, overlaying them across their team and its future requirements. They are:

1. How do we ensure we recruit the most able people?

2. How do we ensure we retain our most valuable people?

3. How do we ensure we promote our most deserving people?

They seem like obvious questions, but in reality the majority of organisations struggle to do these well and fail to grasp the fundamental importance of ensuring equality of opportunity for everybody against each of these. The fundamental error many teams make is to assume that the individual must bend their life to fit within the defined parameters of the team rather than the organisational culture understanding that people-centric solutions will make it better able to attract and retain the best.

In building and maintaining her team, the leader's objective is to ensure equality of opportunity for all: talent and cultural fit should be the only determinants. But it's easier said than done – and certainly a complacent, 'We do it how we've always done it' approach will rapidly be exposed. Addressing with fresh eyes these three seemingly familiar questions is also enlightened self-interest. If you want to be the best, you need the best people, and if you lose close to 50 per cent of your workforce once they start to have families or you only hire people from narrow sections of society (for example) then you're going to underperform against your potential and increasingly in comparison with others – especially as many are starting to find effective new solutions to these questions.

For example, the gender pay gap that exists in many

organisations is the result of failures in the retention and promotion of senior women. Understanding this allows the creation of focused strategies and actions to reduce the gap. It's obvious stuff, but so often misunderstood or simply avoided.

In practice, for many people today at various stages of their career, a one-size-fits-all approach puts them at a significant disadvantage – for example:

- those who are not from the 'right' backgrounds when applying for entry-level jobs (try removing school and university from application forms to encourage a wider range of applicants – and weed out unconscious bias from the recruitment end)

- those who are not easily able to work a five-day, 8.30 a.m. to 6.00 p.m. working week (for example, new parents)

- those who look after an aging relative

- those who want to be able to work from home more during their child's exam year.

The smart leader recognises not only that finding solutions to these kind of questions is the right thing to do, but that it is in their interests to do so. It makes them a more attractive employer, ensures that they retain more of their best people and allows the very best to rise to the very top – the ultimate meritocracy.

Equality of opportunity is critical to a long-term healthy team. Great teams are meritocracies made up of the best-skilled and most motivated members. More than ever, the best people look into the culture and environment they will be joining – and, having joined, will regularly compare it to those of competitors. Having effective strategies against these three questions helps the leader design a people-centric culture built around the needs of her most valuable assets – and helps her team members live their whole lives. It would be a brave leader who claimed that they consistently performed brilliantly at all three, and yet it is a prize well worth striving for. A team that focuses hard on finding great answers will be a team few would ever want to leave. It's a classic example of leadership being difficult, but not complicated.

As with much of leadership, the start point is to be aware. The second is to understand the problem. The third is to have a clearly structured plan and the final – and as always most important: do stuff.

The leader should be looking at her teams and asking herself the three questions (recruit, promote or retain) to ensure, as far as is possible, that opportunities are equal, and that the environment and culture can be shaped to suit the varied lives of her key talent – both the talent she employs today and the talent she'd like to employ tomorrow.

The array of permutations and options open to her are many and varied, but the biggest barrier a leader will face is not coming up with intelligent solutions to the problems she finds, but being prepared to step up and take the necessary actions to solve them. Doing stuff, especially when it challenges a well-established status quo, is always the hardest part of the job.

The leader must act as a shield to give confidence and protection to their team

No leader leads in a vacuum; no team exists in isolation. Everyone reading this has a task they want their team to perform, and all wish to improve that performance (preferably rapidly) over time. Everyone has customers, clients and competitors that define in large part the task they are trying to fulfil. It is tempting (and common) to talk of leadership as a solo act that is conducted in splendid isolation from the world around – the world of internal politics, competing teams and the million other vagaries that impact our very human lives – but the purpose of this book is to enable real-world leadership and real-world solutions.

If the world looks messy and complicated for you, the leader, how must it feel to those who work for you? Of course, a primary task of the leader is to bring clarity, and it is because the world is messy and imperfect that I have urged throughout this book that you choose simple, ambitious objectives, removing the extraneous and focusing on action. However, a No Bullshit Leader knows that despite their best efforts, organisations can be disorienting places.

Consider the leader's role in two parts: the internal and external. We have spent much of this book so far focused on what I consider to be the internal aspects of leadership. These are defining objectives, culture and strategy; identifying key individuals; and building teams. However, the leader must also focus on the world outside the team she creates. She must focus on the external forces that will, without her careful management, pull her team apart.

There is little point in devoting and effort to create clear strategies and culture if you don't work equally hard to avoid these being derailed by external forces, and the world beyond your team (from inside your wider organisation and outside it) will continually do its level best to do just that.

The effective leader must create a bubble for their team. They must act as a shield that protects their team from outside interference. The leader is a punchbag who must absorb input, ideas and blows from all sides, carefully filtering or even blocking these from her team or organisation if she feels they will distract. She must shield her team from distractions and relentlessly keep their eyes on the prize. A successful leader must be like Captain America – sheltering his team behind his shield.

A simple way of doing this is by asking yourself: do your team know and believe that you've got their back? (My editor hated this Americanism, but I blocked this outside interference.) It's a simple question, but a demanding one for a leader. Nobody would want the answer to be no, yet we've all been in situations where the honest answer is far from clear – indeed where it's pretty obvious that nobody has anybody's back, least of all 'the leader'.

Remember: teams need well defined objectives and priorities; the most effective teams comprise motivated, high-talent individuals whose roles are clear; effective teams deliver against their objectives. The leader must create and then maintain this clarity of focus in a world of continual distractions and setbacks.

If the unity of the team crumbles due to outside actors pulling it in different directions (even with the best intentions) then the result will be a lack of focus, insecurity and doubt. To lead successfully, it isn't sufficient to plan and execute well within the confines of your perimeter; you must also ensure that your teams are protected and insulated from external factors that if left unchecked will derail your strategy. This requires of the leader single-mindedness and even bloody-mindedness.

Your teams must know that you unambiguously have their back, that you will fight and strive to maintain the culture, the objectives and the strategy that you have collectively agreed.

A health warning here is that, if it isn't already obvious, leadership is not a popularity contest. The determined protection of a team's integrity and focus can sometimes make a leader unpopular, but the goal is the point. Saying no can sometimes be the hardest, but most effective thing you can do. And the best way you can contribute is by building and maintaining a team that delivers results – if you do that, everything else is just noise.

How not to hire great people

I often talk to company leaders who describe with great pride the complexity of their talent-selection process: how many hoops, hurdles and backflips a candidate must make before being selected. Often I'll hear of businesses that insist that a candidate meet eight, nine or ten people before selection. My god, I think to myself, you're telling me this as evidence of how seriously you take it and therefore how good you are at it. I, on the other hand, just think you are unable to make a decision.

I have directly hired hundreds of people throughout my career, and have come to believe – not just based on my own successes (or lack thereof) but also in observing others – that if, out of every three people you hire, one turns out to be a fantastic success, one does just fine, and one somewhat disappoints, then you are doing pretty well. Do better than this and you're above par; worse and it's no disgrace. Hiring is an art rather than a science, and I see no correlation between the amount of time taken to make a decision (and in this example the amount of opinions canvassed) and the likelihood of the decision being a good one. I use hiring as an example, but I would broaden that observation to many other aspects of daily life.

It's also important to remember that when meeting the best people you are both buying and selling. They have choices (perhaps more choices than you), and if your process suggests sluggishness or indecision you're going to lose out. Just like everything else in your team, how you hire is both a way of shaping your culture and, for the candidate, a signifier of your culture. If you don't see it as an opportunity for competitive advantage, or conversely aren't aware of the disadvantages of doing it badly, then you're going to lose out to somebody who does it better.

If you don't back yourself and you don't back the people around you to make good decisions when hiring, get people you do trust. It's as simple as that.

Removing the wrong people can be as transformative as hiring the right ones

'Your greatest assets get in the lift at the end of the day' – is there a more mindless cliché in the language of business? It's a crowded field, I admit.

People are complicated, all of us: the people we work for, the people who work for us; our customers, our peers and our families. And it is easy to forget that at different points in our day all of us are all of the above: we are all bosses, members of teams, customers, clients, family members and peers – all at the same time.

A successful leader must build teams out of these complicated beings, and the acid test of his success is that under his leadership these teams must outperform their competitors; they must sustain changes of behaviour that are new to them, and they must continually shift and evolve as circumstances change. This is the leader's challenge.

The No Bullshit Leader therefore must add some important caveats to the above cliché. He agrees that his greatest assets get in the lift at the end of the day, and he will spend many hours worrying about how to keep these people motivated and feeling rewarded. However, he would also add that, yes, his greatest assets get into the lift, but also some of his greatest liabilities.

There is little point, it seems to me, in talking of talent and teams if we don't also address the elephant in the room, that for many leaders determining who are her greatest liabilities and removing those who are in the way is a major physical and emotional challenge, as well as often being the single biggest barrier to change. Business books rarely talk about the transformative effect on a business of removing people, but all leaders know it's true. The problem is, it is something of a taboo subject. It happens all the time, yet so many organisations and leaders hide it, and avoid talking about it. Business books focus all their efforts on 'talent', and little time on some of the more uncomfortable aspects of creating a world-class team.

A notable exception is a freely available document produced by Netflix entitled, 'Netflix Culture: Freedom & Responsibility'. It's very long, and I cannot say I agree with it all, but even as a thought piece it provides an unusual and provocative approach to creating a respectful and yet high-performing environment. Google it and form your own view. A key point it makes is the uncomfortable-obvious truth: great cultures and great teams need to remove people as well as hire them.

A common reason for avoiding this subject is that it makes people (the very people you want to feel liberated and energised) feel insecure and scared. I admit it's a risk, but let's briefly consider the issue from a different perspective. Meet Jake.

Jake is a senior member of your team. He knows his stuff, but people don't like working with him and he has poor retention of people within his team. He appears to be enthusiastic about your strategy, but whether deliberately or not he is unwilling or unable to face up to the need to change himself despite being good at pointing out the failings of others. However, his customers like and trust him – despite their continual criticism of your wider organisation.

A very real and everyday leadership challenge is: what do you do with Jake? Every team has one.

Jack Welsh was the CEO of General Electric when they were the biggest company in the world (back when making things mattered to stock markets). Welsh was a rock-star CEO of a type largely unknown outside the US. He is, to put it mildly, a controversial figure. He was a hard man, but one who achieved incredible levels of success and inspired great loyalty amongst many who worked for him.

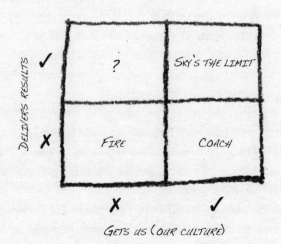

One year, Welsh published the grid shown opposite. It divided people across four boxes and within each were accompanying actions. For two of the groups, he said, the actions are obvious: fire the people who have been grouped in the bottom left, promote those in the top right. However, it's less clear what should be done with the other two groups. Both are familiar and significant challenges for every leader.

For those in the bottom-right box, Welsh thought that these people should be given every chance of succeeding in his businesses. For them he wrote: Coach.

Finally, comes the last box, top left: the box where Jake sits. All companies have people such as this, and they often represent one of the leader's greatest challenges: how to deal with people who deliver results but aren't prepared to work within the culture. Welsh, the most hard-nosed of hard-nosed businessmen, said that he had found time and time again, in businesses of all types right across the world, that teams only began to change once they removed these people. It's a bold position to take.

What Welsh effectively said was that the performance of the whole unit could be accelerated (or conversely held back) by the coherence and consistency of the culture. In fact, to misquote Bill Bernbach, 'a culture's not a culture until it costs you money'. Either you believe a strong and coherent culture is what will drive your team, or you don't.

It is also worth reminding ourselves who in your organisation is most negatively affected by Jake on a day-to-day basis – not necessarily you as the leader, that's for sure. The leader rarely if ever experiences first-hand the consequences of those who behave badly in their organisation. In fact, this can make finding them and rectifying their behaviours very difficult. The leader does not experience being bullied, does not see somebody taking credit for the work of others, does not end up staying late into the evening to make up for those who trail in mid-morning with a predictable litany of excuses.

The leader is often cocooned from these day-to-day frustrations. In fact, often these people are also very good at managing upwards – we've all had the wool pulled over our eyes from time to time. The people who suffer the most are exactly those who the leader most wants to liberate, the people who have to work with Jake day to day. It is they who end up demoralised, and they who feel that the leader's fine words about culture are so much hot air, because Jake can do whatever he likes as long as his client is happy (or at least, happy with him). Culture is the behaviour of management, and if Jake is allowed to do as he pleases, then the management's real sentiments are only too clear. As Bernbach actually said, 'a principle is only a principle if it costs you money'.

In the short-term dealing with Jake is painful, difficult and may even cost you money (although in my experience often less than you'd think), but until you do, your culture will never truly change. And if it comes to it, far from being upset, the people who work with him will rejoice. It's their working lives you'll transform more than your own, and in this small transformation lies a real and powerful step towards significant cultural change. This is the real lesson of Jack Welsh's grid.

I have presented this grid many times to all sorts of groups of people, and it is safe to say that for the vast majority (at all levels), a slide where the word 'fire' appears elicits an initial involuntary recoil not dissimilar to watching a hypodermic injection. This is understandable, however I believe that in order to create a high-performing team, we must be able to have an adult discussion about the career benefits for everyone who is part of it. The leader must not be capricious, malicious or indeed exhibit Jake's behaviours herself, rather they must be direct and honest about the values and behaviours they believe are critical to the success of the enterprise. They must create a culture, as with the British Olympic Team (see Chapter 4), that is owned by everyone, and to which the organisation holds itself accountable. In that environment, there is no debate or dispute about what must ultimately happen to those who refuse to take part.

Does it make those people bad people? Of course not. We have all worked with people who have been a poor fit in one organisation only to thrive in another. But as a leader, that's not your concern. You must be clear with your team and be clear on the culture and behaviours required to succeed. These behaviours and values are not yours; they belong to the team, and the team owns them because good teams want to succeed.

How to have difficult conversations – and making sure you have them

How many things are on your to-do list that you know you should tackle, but have been putting off? Some of the most successful leadership books in the world, multi-million-copy sellers, are basically long-form instructions telling you not to put off the difficult tasks on your list, but rather to tackle them first. However, the reality is we all delay actioning the difficult stuff – I can think of several such items on my own list right now. And for many of us, the trickiest and most commonly avoided task is having that difficult conversation.

Of course, there are very different grades of difficult conversations, but most of us from time to time dodge them and fudge them. Building teams involves talking to people continuously, formally and informally, about what you think, what they think, how you're doing and how they're doing. An excellent book, *The One Minute Manager*, is a great and quick read on the subject.

The best advice I ever received about having difficult conversations was to Just Fucking Do It. Often there is no way to gild the lily, but people agonise about how best to say things that they themselves find uncomfortable. A point to remember here is that all of us are discomforted by different things, but typical topics might be feeding back to a direct report, dealing with a difficult client or asking for a pay rise or promotion. (As a side note, you'll be surprised how often people's reactions are far from what you expect, even if they really don't like what you have to say.) Whatever the reaction, to get there you have to find a beginning, and ultimately the best way is to force yourself to bite the bullet – to just get started, however inelegantly.

Of course, if you can make a point eloquently, that is all the better, but for many of us our concern that we can't is used as an excuse to not have the conversation at all. Which is the worst possible outcome. An honest, if awkward, conversation can transform relationships, performance and satisfaction for all concerned. Often just the act of saying what's on your mind can open up a line of discussion that removes barriers to performance that you didn't even know were there: there is rarely one side to any situation.

A good leader has a good and open dialogue with their team, and encourages their team to have a good and open dialogue with them and each other. If difficult things need to be said, it is far preferable to just sit down and begin, even if your language is clumsy, than to have no conversation at all – and you'll be surprised how often a better conversation and outcome will ensue once you get the ball rolling.

A common concern is that in the heat of the moment people fear they won't be able to clearly express the points they want to make. One simple way to prepare is to take a little time in advance to write down what it is you want to say. This cannot replicate the to and fro of talking to someone, but it can be very effective neverthe-less, and has the dual effect of both helping you marshal your thoughts and making you feel more confident. It's certainly an awful lot easier than trying to think clearly when your palms are sweating and your mouth is dry. In fact, in many circumstances it is perfectly acceptable for you to take these notes with you into the conversation – make a virtue of it. This works one on one, in groups, when speaking in public (of course) and on the telephone.

Each situation will be unique, but ensuring you are able to calmly and clearly say what you want or need to say is common to all of them. Whether you achieve your meeting objective is a whole different matter, but at the very least you will leave the room happy that you've expressed your point in a clear and professional manner. There's nothing worse than working out exactly what and how you should have said something after the event (we've all been there, right?). The time taken to prepare will never be time wasted, and writing down what you want to say – in simple, clear, polite but direct language – is an easy way to make sure you get your point across. Use colleagues, mentors and friends to help get your message and delivery right.

A conversation, of course, involves at least two parties who often have very different perspectives, but what is for sure is that a clumsy but clear beginning is better than no beginning at all. Without the right conversations, progress will be difficult.

Talent on loan

Let's not kid ourselves: really great people are difficult to find. It's also fair to say that in most cases the same person can perform very differently in different teams and environments. This is a good thing, and gives hope to us all – it is also a practical demonstration of the power (for good or bad) of culture.

There are however a few, shining stars who we all want in our team. These people are rare, exciting and can transform a team's performance seemingly single-handed.

As a leader you should of course search out and treasure these people, but you must also be realistic. Great talent is only ever on loan. Too often team leaders forget that everyone has a choice, and the more talented people are, the more choices they have. These people stay because they want to – and as soon as they don't, you have a problem.

There exists in many employers a belief that they are the ones in positions of power, as they are the ones making the decisions during the hiring process. In reality, if you want to attract the very best, you are more often selling than buying: the best have many choices, and if you as leaders or employers don't perform, they will vote with their feet. And there is nothing that undermines the performance of a team more quickly than the departure of key talent (in my experience this can be far more drastic than the departure of even the biggest customer). Yet most leaders spend much more time worrying about the satisfaction of their key customers than they do their key people. They would be wise to remember that in today's world, talent is every bit as fluid as customers.

The smart leader knows who their key talent is, and

they know not just whether they are happy or satisfied in the instant, but understand more broadly what their medium-term (or longer) ambitions are. The better you understand this, the better able you are to ensure that you help meet these. And at least if there comes a point where you can't, you are prepared in advance. If talented people are going to leave, you want them to leave as friends, with a clear and successful structure behind them – unlike as is so often the case, a brutal divorce, with both parties desperate to cause as much harm to the other as possible; that way both lose.

Ultimately, too many employers and leaders behave as though people 'belong' to them. It is one that allows and facilitates the fulfilment of the ambitions of its people and encourages an equality of the relationship between employer and employed – allowing each to gain satisfaction and growth. An effective culture is one that doesn't just deliver for the whole, but draws people to it as a place where they are able to do their best work while there – whether that be for two years or twenty. At the point where ambitions diverge, talent will move on, and new opportunities will arise for new people.

And finally, don't forget the easy conversations

If leaders agonise and take too long over difficult conversations, then they very often forget about the easy ones altogether.

In most teams and for most people the opportunities to lift up and praise others are many times more frequent than the need for the opposite, but leaders so often overlook them.

Positive feedback is the most effective and rewarding way to build the culture you need. The effective leader ensures that in amongst the hubbub and noise she remembers to say 'well done'. Few words are more effective, and few simple acts so frequently overlooked.

To return briefly to Jack Welsh, he habitually wrote notes of praise to his direct reports – right around the world. Across his long career Welsh is reputed to have written thousands of such notes – and so valued and prized were they by his teams, many report having kept them to this day.

Saying thank you gets stuff done.

EVEN LESS BULLSH*T

5

BEING FOLLOWED

Most organisations are just buildings full of people.
What makes one better than the other? Talent
and culture.

Great culture alone may make a good team, but
without great talent you won't ever be the best.

⇩

We're all in the talent acquisition business:

*How good are you for the careers of the people who
work for you?*

⇩

A great team is comprised of great individuals who
see the fulfilment of the team's objectives as wholly
aligned with the fulfilment of their own ambitions.

⇩

Great teams need stolid professionals and maverick
playmakers – and a culture that values both equally.

Diverse teams win.

Equality of opportunity is achieved by asking:
How do we:

- recruit the most able people?
- retain our most valuable people?
- promote our most deserving people?

The leader must act as a shield to give confidence
and protection to their team.

Removing the wrong people can be as
transformative as hiring the right ones.

⬇

Make sure you're not shirking the difficult
conversations (and nor is your team) …
nor forgetting the easy ones: saying thank you gets
stuff done.

6

ENERGY AND RESILIENCE

There is no better than adversity. Every defeat, every heartbreak, every loss contains its own seed, its own lesson on how to improve your performance next time.

Malcolm X

IT'S EASY IN A BOOK such as this to blithely say, as I have more than once, that the way to become a better leader is to become more comfortable with the possibility, or even inevitability, of error and failure. It's easy for me to write it and easy for you to nod reading it as you munch crisps on a train. The reality when it strikes, however, is often anything but – and all leaders must be able to deal with the hard times, getting through them and thriving despite them. Because as a leader, the one thing you can be sure of is that tough times will come.

Leading is hill-climbing and it's persuading others that the climb is worthwhile

Leading is like standing at the bottom of a valley: hills rise to every side; only the road behind you snakes back down.

For a leader every forward route always heads uphill. Hill-climbing can be an exhilarating and rewarding experience, but it is tough – this is how leadership always feels.

A great leader gets her team to a place where they can see the summit, but are never quite there. As soon as you feel you're at the top – the only way (literally and emotionally) is down. Leading is hill-climbing, and it's persuading others that the climb is worthwhile. It's making sure they're safe, picking them up when they stumble, re-energising them when they slow, making them believe when they doubt. It is taking your team over rise after rise, and just as everybody thinks you're done, pointing to the summit in the distance and saying, let's do that one next.

As with leadership, there are many skills required for a hill-climber, but only one that is indispensable: the preparedness to work really fucking hard. To return again to Mike Brearley, who quotes the influential British theatre director Katie Mitchell:

> *Ninety-eight per cent of what the director does is hard work. There is a prevalent idea that directors spend their time sitting around at dinner parties, or going for a walk in the park to get new insights. If only it were so, this romantic view. In fact this amounts to perhaps 2 per cent of what I do, when there is a moment of new insight into the material which will help articulate it in a stimulating way to the audience; but I never rely on it, and would never assume it's there. Each morning you get up and do more work on the text.*

Opportunity looks a lot like hard work – or, life lessons from Ashton Kutcher

In 2013 Ashton Kutcher accepted yet another teen award in front of a huge crowd of adoring fans. After shushing the assembled masses, he gave a short, but unexpectedly memorable speech on life. It's far from clear that anybody in the audience paid it the slightest bit of attention, and I'm not sure how I initially discovered it, but it's definitely worth watching.

He starts by telling his fans that his real name isn't Ashton, it's Chris, and he wants to talk to them about life lessons he learned back when he was still plain Chris.

Here is what he had to say about hard work:

> When I was 13 I had my first job helping my dad carrying shingles up to the roof.
> And then I got a job washing dishes at a restaurant.
> And then I got a job in a grocery store deli.
> And then I got a job in a factory sweeping Cheerio dust off the ground.
> And I've never had a job in my life I was better than.
> I was always just lucky to have a job.
> And every job I had was a stepping-stone to my next job, and I never quit my job until I had my next job.
> And so opportunities look a lot like work.

As we learn from Ashton/Chris, for all of us, opportunities look a lot like hard work. Hard work is also a *leitmotif* that runs through the words and deeds of great leaders. However, the right question to ask of yourself is: how do I ensure I'm getting a return on all my effort? After all, although we may acknowledge hard work as leadership table-stakes, it is still very easy to waste your effort if you're not careful, deliberate and (dare I say it) strategic.

An experienced team knows that the road ahead will be bumpy and difficult, and that no matter how great the effort and how strong your skills, success is never guaranteed. What's more, even if you're successful, some work will be wasted; you just don't know in advance which bits. The trick is not to bemoan this waste – it's inevitable – but rather to be self-aware enough to reduce it as much as you possibly can through having a clear and universally understood objective and strategy. Consider this waste-reduction process as the Return on Pain (R.O.P. – as opposed to Return on Investment, although that kind of works too). It's an acknowledgement that the process may be just as painful whether you succeed or fail, win or lose. However, if successful, the high R.O.P. will make that pain worthwhile. If unsuccessful ... well, things won't feel quite as great.

We can all think of projects large or small where this rule applies. In my industry most growth comes through winning pitches – or in crude terms, learning to steal our competitors' clients. It's dog-eat-dog, and many companies, big and small, work in the same way. The pitching process can be a brutally tough and draining experience, but one that successful businesses need to master in order to thrive. I have taken part in many pitches, some fabulous and some disastrous. There is, however, little difference between the two in terms of the effort expended – the pain. Pitches are like a Formula 1 race: the stakes are very high, they cost a lot of money, the teams involved are large and complicated, and at their conclusion the margins between success and failure are wafer thin. Unlike Formula 1 however, no points are awarded for second place. All pitching is about winning, and the first question I always ask is, 'Are we prepared to do what it takes to win?' It's a non-trivial question. It requires first of all working out what is *really* required (this is often not an easy question) and then, whether we are able and willing to do that.

As with much else related to leadership, that all seems obvious, right? But in reality, I find that the answers to these questions are not obvious, nor are they always answered honestly. It is another example of the difference between 'being right' and 'winning'. Pitching is nothing to do with being right; it is everything to do with winning.

To return then to the R.O.P.: first, teams should demand that if they are to put in the necessary level of effort that a good pitch requires, then they firstly must align on what it will take to win; and second, they should ensure that they are prepared to do that thing. This gives a chance of a high R.O.P. If they aren't prepared (or able) to do it – then walk away, get your weekends back and save your energy for next time. Losing a pitch is a very low R.O.P.

We must keep our R.O.P. as high as possible, and to do that we have to be laser focused on how and why we are expending our effort. As we all know, it's very easy to fill your time (or worse, have your time filled for you by others), but far harder to make sure someone is paying you well in return.

The mundanity of excellence

However, we don't *just* want opportunities (although we do want opportunities, and lots of them), nor do we want to be drones slaving studiously away, without direction or reward. We want a consistently high R.O.P.; we want to be the best and we want our teams to be the best. We want talented people in talented teams, but what actually is talent and how do we get it?

Hamilton College professor Daniel Chambliss spent eighteen months with a group of swimmers trying to find the answer. He set out a definitive study of what it takes to be world-class – and how those who are world-class performers differ from the rest of us mere mortals. In doing so, he coined a fabulous phrase which, in its backhanded sort of way, should give hope to us all: the 'mundanity of excellence'.

He chose swimming because the differences between success and failure are so clearly delineated and so tiny, often milliseconds. In such an environment he was able to minutely analyse the differences between the merely good and the great.

His three findings make for fascinating, counter-intuitive and thought-provoking reading:

1. 'Talent' is a story we tell ourselves to explain the performance of others

'The concept of talent hinders a clear understanding of excellence ... Excellence is not, I find, the product of ... deviant personalities.'

In other words, those incredible, graceful beings we see gliding effortlessly from one end of the pool to the other are not superhumans at all. We imbue them with other-worldly gifts to excuse our own unwillingness to put in the effort that has got them to that level of perfection. We too could be them, he tells us, we just choose not to be. 'Talent' is an excuse we use to explain not our own inabilities, but our own unwillingness.

2. Learn to love the game, not the results

'At the higher levels something of an inversion of attitude takes place [between those in the A grade and those in the C grade]. What others see as boring and repetitive say, they [the A grade] find peaceful, even meditative, challenging or therapeutic. It is incorrect to believe that top athletes suffer great sacrifices to achieve their goals … they don't see what they do as sacrificial at all. They like it.'

In fact, for them the journey itself may be the thing, rather than the end objective. Those who follow online influencer and entrepreneur Gary Vaynerchuk will be familiar with the sentiment. In his regular posts he urges his millions of followers never to focus on the winning or losing, but to accept both as equal and necessary parts of growing and learning. Vaynerchuk gamifies the journey, as with a sport, telling us that to endure and thrive you must learn to love the activity itself rather than simply the dopamine hits of the victories. For him, the ultimate win is to learn to love 'the game'. What might be considered a hard, stressful grind by some is simply playing the game to him.

3. Excellence is the consistent performance of multiple mundane actions

'Superlative performance is really a confluence of dozens of small skills or activities, each one learned or stumbled upon, which have been carefully drilled into habit and then are fitted together in a synthesised whole. There is nothing extraordinary or superhuman in any one of those actions; only the fact that they are done consistently and correctly, and all together, produce excellence.'

What we perceive as exceptional talent is actually the accumulation of many tiny, quite ordinary actions and skills which when performed simultaneously, give the illusion of unattainable and innate ability.

Excellence then, finds Chambliss, comes from hard work, along with an acceptance, even enjoyment of the process (which those who are less successful feel are chores or impositions) and then, ultimately, the consistent and simultaneous performance of a multitude of individually ordinary skills.

Chambliss's conclusions are powerful on a personal level, as we strive to be better leaders ourselves, and also as we consider how we help others achieve their ambitions and goals – and of course as we build world-class teams. Those we perceive to be talented are different, but not in the way we suppose. Rather they differ in their dedication, their enjoyment of the process and their accumulation and execution of many, many micro-skills. They aren't born able to do it, so you shouldn't in any way be despondent or discouraged because you weren't either. Nobody was. They learnt it just like you can.

It is for sure a counter-intuitive claim, but one we should all embrace with gusto – or at least those of us who wish to be the best version of ourselves. For as Chambliss says, it really could be you.

We want our teams to comprise radiators not drains – people who transform a team's mood when they walk into a room

Leaders lead teams – and though teams are comprised of individuals, they are different, more complicated organisms than any of those individuals on their own. The successful leader must understand and manage their own and their team's growth (towards excellence), and a critical part of that is managing your collective energy levels. Achieving greatness is hard work, but the successful leader recognises how draining this can be if the results don't appear quickly, or if the team dynamic isn't working. A team must be able to maintain and develop its energy levels to carry it through the periods where the R.O.P. feels low – or simply through a long night before a big meeting the following morning. This cannot only be the responsibility of the leader – she must build a team that can self-sustain and self-recharge.

We've all been in the room late at night, the strip lights frazzling brains, cold coffee and old pizza boxes on the table, tempers fraying and the deadline looming. In walks Adam. What happens to the mood – does the mood lift or sink? Is Adam a radiator or a drain?

If I'm choosing a heart surgeon or a pilot then I'm not too bothered about her personality, but I am very, very interested in her skillset. However, for many roles today, attitude massively outpunches skills. For many roles – including often the most highly paid and responsible, the functional parts of a job just aren't that difficult to learn. What is very difficult to replace is experience, and what's hard to train is attitude. The people we want in our teams are people who bring energy, whatever their job title or background. It's the lifeblood of a successful team culture.

Drains take away a group's energy. They may be bright, driven, ambitious and they may even be right, but they sap the life from a team. They sponge the energy from others; when they enter a room the mood worsens – the elusive answer edges further away.

Radiators energise a room. One of the most fabulous people I ever worked with was exactly this person. Sheryl instinctively knew her role within the team, and more than that, understood what the team needed in order to make it work. What this meant in practise was that she recognised that for every team her role would change, because each team needed different things to make them whole. It's worth pausing on this for a moment, because although it is fairly obvious, it is rare that people are able (or prepared) to do this. Most of us struggle to play one role well – never mind more than one. This isn't of course to say that she could or would be able to fill all roles herself, but she recognised the bits that weren't working and found ways to fix them – or found someone who could.

A team is a complicated organism designed to complete a given task. The task, not the team, is the objective. Sheryl understood that, and was prepared to do the things that needed to be done to make the team whole.

Sometimes it was carrot; sometimes it was stick. (I am reminded here of the foul-mouthed spin doctor Malcolm Tucker from *The Thick of It*. 'I plan to use a carrot and stick approach,' he assures his acolytes. 'I'm going to hit him with the stick and stick the carrot up his arse.') Sometimes that was a stern talking to; sometimes when everybody was working late and spirits were dropping it was, 'Does anybody fancy a cup of tea?' People loved her. People loved having her in the room, and when she opened the door and walked in, the answer edged a little closer. Sheryl was the ultimate radiator – it got cold when she left.

To understand why is not just to understand that positive energy trumps negative energy, it is to understand the power of individual attitude in making teams work. Some of the most valuable team members I've ever worked with have been the most junior. They are people who instinctively know how to be the glue that binds the egos and insecurities into a formidable whole. They don't do the sexy stuff that people write case studies about, like creativity and strategy. They do the often unnoticed and unseen stuff that allows the time, space and security for others to shine. They are people who instinctively recognise the talents of the others in the team and, like water flowing across a cracked floor, simply fill the spaces that others don't.

We want our teams to be comprised of radiators, not

drains. We want people who when they walk in the room immediately make everybody feel better, not worse.

The leader must be like the Duracell bunny, still banging the drum long after the others have toppled over

As the leader you must be the radiator-in-chief. If you've had a bad morning, you can't sit at your desk with your head in your hands. You can't scream and shout and moan 'woe is me'. You must find the balance between authenticity and being a predictable and reliable beacon of stability and certainty. Your team look to you, and if you appear lost, they feel lost; if you appear disheartened, they too will lose heart. The challenge, of course, is that you also must be human, and humans have emotions. Pretending setbacks don't matter can be as damaging as overreacting. The great leader must be able to walk the tightrope Kipling described in his famous poem 'If': '[to] meet with Triumph and Disaster / And treat those two impostors just the same'.

Returning again to Brearley, this time quoting the acclaimed film director Stephen Frears: '[the leader must have] The ability to be present and absent at the same time, being able to function and contribute in the day-to-day, of being in charge, whilst simultaneously being able to step outside of this and see and feel the bigger picture; the broader landscape within which they are acting.'

In a way, so much, so obvious, but it's really tough to do.

In the film *The Revenant* Leonardo DiCaprio's character

goes through an almost comically horrifying set of misadventures, accidents, betrayals and attacks. It is a Homeric-scale story of betrayal, trial and nemesis. As a leader you fortunately don't often have to flee vengeful Native American tribes, jump your horse off a cliff or fight angry bears, but sometimes a day, a week or a month can feel a little more like DiCaprio's plight than it does the slick certainties of *The Social Network*.

Leading can be draining because, ironically, being a radiator is draining. The leader must, if necessary, be like the Duracell bunny, still banging the drum long after the others have toppled over. However, all of us only have so much energy to give, which is why we instinctively value so highly those with whom we can share the burden and who help us recharge. Teams without energy sources quickly fade and die.

Failures are inevitable, and you can't succeed if you don't find ways to brush these off, pick yourself up and keep going

Talent is energy and energy is talent. All of us can have it, but a leader must jealously protect her store, share it wisely and search out others and opportunities to help her recharge. It is impossible to lead without falling down, and the obvious corollary is that it is impossible to lead without being able to dust yourself off and get back to your feet. The Chinese have an expression that succinctly captures the winning leader's attitude:

Fall down seven times, stand up eight.

The Swiss tennis player Stan Wawrinka has Samuel Beckett's rather more poetic version tattooed on the inside of his left forearm so that it is in his eyeline every time he serves:

> *Ever tried. Ever failed. No matter. Try again. Fail again.*
> *Fail better.*

Failures are inevitable, setbacks happen and you cannot progress if you don't find ways to brush these off, pick yourself up and get going again. Talk to anybody in any walk of life from authors and actors to entrepreneurs and sportspeople about how they made it and they will tell you first of the hardships, of the rejections, the late nights and much worse. Ultimately, great achievement is impossible without great resilience. Leadership is the continuous climb uphill, and without a degree of bloody-mindedness you're never going to get to the top (or the top of the next hill, and the one after that …). If hard work is leadership's physical expression, resilience is its mental equivalent.

If leading doesn't hurt (at least some of the time) then you're not doing it right. A leader must make decisions in order to create action: making decisions sufficient to impact the organisation means getting stuff wrong sometimes, upsetting people, failing and beginning again.

For me the hardest period of my career was my first six years as a managing director – a period in which we failed and failed again, to the extent that I genuinely (with good reason) believed that I had ruined my career. Eventually, my luck turned – when all else was failing, resilience got me through (although only just). However, today those six years of failure are the most useful of my career – if nothing else I tell myself, I am determined to never make those same mistakes again.

Getting stuff wrong is necessary to progress, but at the same time tough for the leader and often the team. However obvious and easy this may be to write down, in the real world the personal consequences are hard. Nobody likes to be wrong, and some missteps and problems can have significant, real-world implications – which the leader needs to ensure don't deflate, demoralise or derail her and her team.

Great achievement is impossible without great resilience

Resilience, grit, thick skin – call it what you like, but the successful leader needs it in abundance. To finish with another actor, my favourite perspective on the attitude of the winning leader comes, somewhat unexpectedly, from Will Smith:

> *The only thing that I see that is distinctly different about me is that I'm not afraid to die on a treadmill. You might have more talent than me. You might be smarter than me. You might be sexier than me. You might be all of those things, you got it on me in nine categories. But if we get on the treadmill together, there's two things: you're getting off first, or I'm gonna die. It's really that simple.*

Leadership is that. With a smile on your face.

EVEN LESS BULLSH*T

6

ENERGY AND RESILIENCE

Leading is hill-climbing, and it's persuading others
that the climb is worthwhile.

Opportunities look a lot like hard work.

The mundanity of excellence:

- Talent is a story we tell ourselves to explain the
performance of others.

- Learn to love the 'game' not the results.

- Excellence is the consistent performance of
multiple mundane actions.

We want our teams to comprise radiators not drains
– people who transform a team's mood when they
walk into a room.

The leader must be like the Duracell bunny, still banging the drum long after the others have toppled over.

Failures are inevitable, and you can't succeed if you don't find ways to brush these off, pick yourself up and keep going.

Great achievement is impossible without great resilience.

7

LEADING YOURSELF

Know thyself.

Socrates

SUCCESS REQUIRES SIGNIFICANT commitment of a leader over a prolonged period of time. In earlier chapters I sketched out my manifesto for how a leader might best spend that time, and that in addition, you must possess an abundance of energy and resilience, be persistent and own a rhino-like hide. These attributes, however, come at a price. Recognising and managing this is essential to your longevity. Becoming and remaining a successful leader requires that you look after yourself – that you have yourself on your to-do list. Pretty close to the top.

In just the same way that you must assume that nobody is going to care about your career as much as you do, ultimately nobody cares as much about your successes as you do, nor will anyone else ensure that you keep the different parts of your life in balance. That's not cynical, it's just realistic – and it's mostly because others are too busy dealing with their own shit to have much time to deal with yours. In fact – it would be odd if it were otherwise. That's not to say nobody cares – far from it. But if you assume you have to look after yourself, then you're not going to go far wrong. And at least you'll be sure that someone you know and trust is on the case.

You matter – and being a leader is tough. It's easy to write it down, easy to smile at Will Smith's views on running machines, but here we should pause, because to succeed you must ensure you are fit to lead. I have striven to avoid the clichés of the leadership industry thus far, and hesitate slightly as I write those words, but having typed them, closed my computer, walked round the block, come back and read them again – I think cliché or not, it's a subject we must tackle. Because if we don't look after ourselves and if you're not prioritising you – no amount of airport books, coaches and resilience are going to help. Without considering yourself as a project to be developed and worked on you will ultimately fall short. And who wants that? We don't just want to survive, we want to thrive – to be effective, to act, to be resilient, to grow and, in amongst all this, to enjoy ourselves.

As we discussed in Chapter 6, your energy is not an infinite resource; even the Duracell bunny tires eventually. Your resilience, no matter how great, is not unbreakable. To lead well, to thrive and grow, you must first follow Socrates' injunction from the Athenian agora – 'know thyself'.

The successful leader must be a selfish leader: she must take as much care of herself as she does of others

A great leader isn't just somebody who has one lucky bounce. A great leader is somebody who has a long and successful career, each step on their journey building on the last. Sure, they'll have knocks, but they have the resilience, will and passion to go on. When we think of our own real-life examples of those 'knocks', we remember just how painful and debilitating they can be. They aren't so easy to dust off when it's you and when it's happening right now. If we're not careful as leaders, success can come at too high a price. To be a great leader you have to make sure you are fit, healthy and able to continue to succeed well into the future.

The demystification of leadership is ultimately the demystification of the leader. Our histories echo with stories of the heroic leader, the supermen and women who change the course of history: Julius Caesar, Joan of Arc, Elizabeth I, Lincoln, Florence Nightingale, Churchill and many more. They seem to tower above us to such an extent that it becomes almost impossible to imagine them in anything other than the heroic poses we know so well; lamp held aloft, or cigar above jutting chin. However, these caricatures hide the real people and their inevitable 'real people' insecurities, doubts, weaknesses and failures. It isn't that great leaders don't have these feelings; they just are able to deal with them and act anyway. And they find a way to do it time and time again.

Success requires of the leader the ability to sustain not just their team, but crucially their own health, happiness, motivation and belief. It is a reasonable (if somewhat empirical) observation that if leadership is lonely, the greater the responsibility, the greater the sense of isolation. All of us have felt, if perhaps only occasionally, the sense of distance from friends and family that comes at the times of greatest stress and pressure. Just when you most need a release valve it can be most difficult to find.

The successful leader, then, must be a selfish leader. Selfish because in order to be consistently effective she must take as much care of herself as she does of others. Ninety per cent of this book is about how to lead other people. This final 10 per cent is how to lead yourself. Just as the cobbler's children are reputedly the worst shod, so most high-performing leaders are often really bad at looking after themselves. Worse, they don't even consider this as something they should actively pay attention to.

For a culture to be healthy it needs to recover from the busy times through downtime – when you get up, walk away and go home

The first step is to recognise that we must find a balance between the various versions of ourselves: as parents, leaders, siblings, children, friends, students and role models. Without finding this balance we will ultimately fail. The purpose and remit of this book does not extend to the entirety of life (if two millennia of philosophers haven't nailed it I'm sure as hell not going to), but it does extend to ensuring that you don't take yourself for granted.

For the majority of us this doesn't just happen, and requires continuous conscious effort. After all – the solutions to the problems others face are trivial compared to how difficult we find our own. Yet without constant vigilance and effort even the most successful, resilient and high-energy leaders derail or worse, burn out. Resilience alone is not enough. The leader should encourage their team to consider themselves as their most important client – and by extension should treat themselves as their most critical team member. Just as in aircraft safety demonstrations, where passengers are encouraged to fit their own masks before helping others, so the leader must first see to their own mental and physical well-being, as the best way to be able to help those in their team.

In Chapter 4 we discussed the definition and importance of culture as a, if not the, key competitive advantage. By this definition, culture is the means by which the team behaves in order to outperform the competition. Long-term advantage is only possible if that culture allows sustainable high-performance, and, as with all definitions of culture, this starts with the leader. The successful leader is a selfish leader, taking care of themselves as the best way to ensure they remain able to embody the culture and take care of the people within it.

A great example of how the behaviour of the leader can create (or inhibit) a healthy working culture is 'presenteeism'. Teams follow their leader's example – often because they believe there is an expectation for them to do so. If a leader is always in at 8.00 a.m., never leaves before 7.00 p.m. and eats lunch at their desk while doing their emails, then there is a high likelihood that their teams will do the same. For many leaders this may well be an unintended consequence, but nevertheless has the effect of creating an unhealthy culture: as always, the *real* culture of the team is most closely linked to the behaviour of management.

Everybody needs to put in long hours sometimes, but equally, everybody will have periods when they could finish early – and if they can, then they should. For a culture to be healthy it needs the downtime to recover from the busy times. Besides, it is simply healthy and refreshing to be in different places, talking to different people about different things – how much of your best work happens at your desk? The leader must set this example. Effectiveness is not correlated to time at your desk. And guess what, great results require periods of rest as well as effort.

When you are able, get up, walk away, go home. There will be plenty of occasions when you can't, so embrace the moments when you can. Work expands to fit the time available – so limit the time you allow it. If you don't your team won't – and if your team won't then they and you will not perform at your best.

This is of course only one example of many: if you're sick you need to stay at home; if your kids need picking up you need to leave early. And the same is true for your teams.

Learn from the Stoics, that your emotions are detached from external events and therefore are fully within your control

In modern English, to be stoic has come to mean a rather dour fatalism, which in some ways is the opposite of its true and original meaning. The Greek Stoics taught that your emotions are disconnected from external events and are fully within your control. At first viewing this is a simple concept, yet hard to accept.

Epictetus, a former slave and leading early Stoic, put it bluntly:

Sick and yet happy, in peril and yet happy, dying and yet happy, in exile and yet happy, in disgrace and yet happy.

Or, to put it in rather less apocalyptic modern terms, 'furious client yet happy'.

In simple terms, no person or thing can make you unhappy (or feel any other emotion): only you are responsible for your emotions. Only you can decide how you feel and how you respond to whatever comes your way.

Marcus Aurelius, one of the 'good' Roman emperors, wrote extensively on Stoicism. A short version of his philosophy is captured in his classic work, *Meditations*, possibly one of the most widely read books of all time, and one that many people even today (among them some of our most successful leaders) return to time and again. In it he doesn't attempt to change the human condition, our weaknesses, insecurities or self-doubts. Instead, he helps us understand them and to thrive despite them.

This must be the leader's lesson. Marcus Aurelius' most famous insight helps us understand that only we are responsible for our feelings:

Choose not to be harmed – and you won't feel harmed.
Don't feel harmed – and you haven't been.

And he exhorts us to live in the present:

Each of us lives only now, this brief instant. The rest has been lived already or is impossible to see.

In other words, only the present is real. The rest is your emotions.

Your feelings and emotions do not in any way affect the fundamental skill base of your team. Learn to trust your process

In 2014, Johanna Konta was a talented but largely unknown British tennis player. Ranked 146th in the world, with her career seemingly stalled, she was introduced by her coach to Juan Coto – once a gifted junior player himself, but who had since built a twenty-year career as a business performance coach working with high-fliers in industries across the world. Now in his forties, Coto remained a high-ranked amateur player, but his task wasn't to improve Konta's skills.

In 2016 Coto talked to the Press Association about his role: '[I like] to help high achievers like Joanna who work in very demanding environments to perform well and enjoy their profession. When you ask a tennis player what the importance is of the mental side [of the game], they say 70 per cent or higher'.

Coto believed that if it was 70 per cent of your game, perhaps it should be 70 per cent of your practice.

Coto's words come straight from Marcus Aurelius and centuries before even him, the early Stoics. The essence of his philosophy, he explained, 'is to focus only on the things you can control. Not winning, or losing or your ranking, but your effort and your attitude. [This way] you release the pressure of what you can't control'. On court, for Konta, that of course included the point just scored and the point still to come.

In sixteen months Konta rose from a world ranking of 146th to inside the world top 10.

Coto released Konta from her past and her future and freed her to live in the moment. Not that match, or set, or game, or point, but the micro-specifics of each movement and shot. If her opponent hit a better shot or she wasn't good enough, so be it. If her first serve went in the net at match point it carried no more significance than the thousands she hit in practice. He freed her to trust only in her skills and to focus on executing her strategy and her effort, the factors in her control.

At moments of self-doubt you must ground yourself by focusing on the fact that your personal feelings and emotions do not in any way affect the fundamental skill base of your team, nor crucially your own. But allowing yourself or your team to become distracted by events outside of your control will reduce your collective effectiveness. The leader's primary role is not simply to focus on basic skills, but to build context and culture that allows the team to confidently and repeatedly execute their skills under the highest pressure.

At Russia 2018 the England football team, habitual underachievers to the extent that they had become something of a national joke, won a penalty shoot-out for the first time ever at a World Cup. It was a young, inexperienced team led by a manager, Gareth Southgate, whose professional football career had been forever defined by his own European Championship penalty miss some twenty years earlier.

In a penalty shoot-out, a team can do nothing at all about whether their opponents score. It is outside their control – a well-struck penalty is all but unsaveable. The other team's performance then is completely disconnected to your own: just as a golfer plays the course rather than their opponent. In theory. The emotional pressure, however, is formidable.

Southgate, when asked how they had managed at last to win, used a memorable phrase. He said the team ensured that they 'managed the process'. The only part of it in their control was who would take part, what order they would do it in, the walk from the halfway line to the penalty box and the execution of their skill once there. Everything else was noise. Control your process and execute your skill. Rehearse your skill so that if penalties come round, you know that you're taking one, you know in what order and you know where you'll aim. Own your process.

Controlling the process doesn't reduce the pressure,

but it does focus you on the factors that you are able to control. As I have shown through this book, leadership is a skill – and at times of stress it is critical that we stay true to its uncomplicated basic principles. This is why No Bullshit Leadership matters – it gives you a process to trust.

This book is your fallback. It has your back when nobody else does. If nothing else, it says build your self-confidence as a leader through always having a clear and simple leadership philosophy. This is what allows you to manage your process.

Accept the inevitability of self-doubt

Is it possible to be a leader and lack self-belief? If I didn't believe the answer was yes, I wouldn't have written this book. In reality there can be few (if any) leaders who don't experience periods wracked by doubt, insecurity and fear, to the extent that the right question to ask yourself is not how do I remove my doubts, but how do I act despite them.

As with addiction, the first step is acceptance: admit it to yourself, and come to terms with it. I'm Chris Hirst and I'm an insecure leader.

Leadership is about achieving future objectives that are often easy to define but difficult to reach. Periods of self-doubt, fear, worry and loss of confidence are inevitable by-products of this process. Furthermore, a leader may experience these feelings over very long periods of time; it is likely you will never be free from them.

She can find herself caught between being the most visible embodiment of the team, and hence feeling these pressures most keenly, while simultaneously feeling the least able to admit or show what can often be perceived to be weaknesses.

The purpose of this book is not to remove these periods of self-doubt – that is both way beyond my expertise and probably undesirable. Self-doubt is not in itself a bad thing; indeed typically we avoid and (rightly) mistrust those who appear to lack self-doubt, those who are unshakeable in their conclusions and convictions. A leader without doubts is a leader who either hasn't asked the right questions or who misunderstands the task.

This book should encourage you to have the confidence to face up to these demons and act anyway. Even the best drilled of sports teams get butterflies in their stomachs. But despite their nerves, doubts and insecurities (not to mention all the personal baggage they lug around with them, just as you and I do), they take to the field confident in their ability to execute their skills and their plans – even under the most extreme pressure. This is how great teams work. The doubts don't disappear, but their trust in teammates, manager, leader, culture and ultimately strategy, liberates them to perform despite the doubts.

None of which guarantees success, of course. Rather, it aims to guarantee consistency of performance through focusing only on those aspects that are within your control. If the other team plays better, if the referee is bad, if the weather is against you, if your boss makes a dumb call

– there's nothing you can do. So don't give it a moment's thought. Trust in your team's culture and talent – the two factors that remain wholly in your control. As your mum always said, all you can do is do your best – and as is often the case, your mum was right.

Don't be afraid to be vulnerable. It's not a sign of weakness, it's a proof of strength, and without it nothing gets done

Several years ago I had a very big and important client who had hired us to relaunch their well-known high-street brand. The stakes were high for us and her, but fortunately it was one of those agency–client relationships that just clicked. We did great work together – work of which I'm still very proud to this day, and the whole process, though stressful, was exciting and fun. She remains one of the best clients I ever had. But Kat had something else that made her special. I clearly remember sitting in the back of a cab one day with a colleague after a tense and difficult meeting with her, and he remarked, 'You know what – Kat's superpower is her vulnerability.' It's an observation I've thought about often since.

For most of us vulnerability is weakness. We hate the idea of it, and develop all sorts of strategies to avoid or hide it. Vulnerability is the fear of exposing ourselves to the possibility of failure, rejection and shame. Yet without the possibility of a negative outcome we will never attempt anything. The possibility of failure is a prerequisite of success in everything from personal relationships to leadership. The fear many people feel asking somebody on a date is the fear of vulnerability – of opening yourself to rejection and (self-perceived) shame.

In a TED Talk that has been viewed over 35 million times, Professor Brené Brown discusses the difficulties of understanding, and ultimately the power of, vulnerability. She describes our collective desire to make the uncertain certain and our inevitable failure to do so. The way to live, she says, is to embrace vulnerability and stop trying to control and predict – a counter-intuitive injunction to many of us. Contrary to how many of us feel, vulnerability is not weakness, she concludes, it is our most accurate measurement of courage: vulnerability is the birthplace of creativity, innovation and change.

Often as leaders we feel afraid or insecure – vulnerable because we don't know the answer and therefore have a choice to avoid the question or risk being seen to fail. For many leaders this lies at the root of their inability to act. We feel the need to build a shield not just to protect our teams, as described in Chapter 5, but to hide ourselves behind.

My client Kat was strong and successful yet unafraid to share her fears and uncertainties, all of which we too experience but mostly keep well below the surface. It made her human and people loved her for it, but more than that it allowed her to build solid, enduring teams. It wasn't a tactic, or a strategy, it was just her and part of what made her a great leader. More than all that, her vulnerability was a measure of her courage to admit things, ask things and do things that another person would fear made them look silly or weak. Kat's natural comfort with her own vulnerability was key to her achieving her soaring ambition.

I'd like to be better at it. I think you should try it to. It's not a sign of weakness, it's a proof of strength, and without being prepared to be vulnerable, nothing gets done.

Live a whole life – leadership is only one part of our complicated lives. The leader-you can only thrive if the other-yous are given a chance as well

You're a leader, or you want to be a leader. I too want you to be a leader: we need more people like you. But even the most successful are not solely leaders – they are many other things beside. To succeed as a leader you must focus on the rest of your life as well. Leadership is only one part of our complicated lives. One minute you're in charge of the careers and fortunes of 500 people, the next you've dumped that easy forehand into the net playing some precocious seventeen-year-old. Where's your leadership bullshit now?

Parents know this feeling well. You come home from a day of virtuous striving and do your kids give a shit? They just want £20 and a lift to town. You're just mum or dad – a cashpoint / taxi. Parents or not, leaders need other lives. To succeed you need to take care of the rest of you. This isn't some tree-hugging bullshit – it's true.

We're each like the Trivial Pursuit playing pieces, the different part of our lives being both interconnected and unique. It's only when all the pieces are fitted together that we are whole. You can't consider yourself only as a leader – partly because it's not true, but mostly because you'll fail if you don't fill in the other pieces. You can't win at Trivial Pursuit with six of the same colour segments and you can't be a great leader without balancing and building the other parts of your life.

Perhaps it's too hard for you to be vulnerable while leading, so go find somewhere else that isn't so hard. Go learn something you're bad at. Go be humbled by people whose achievements dwarf your own (be that by scale, ambition or sacrifice). Go scream at a football team – then coach your own. Learn a language. Write poetry. Try improvisational theatre. In fact, definitely try improvisational theatre. Go to a lecture on a subject you know nothing about. Read, walk, create, cook, camp, play, laugh. Use other parts of your brain.

This isn't a suggestion. It's an injunction. You can't lead well by only working at leading. As Rudyard Kipling observed, 'What do they know of England who only England know?' You must find places to learn, to recharge, to be vulnerable. All of us are multiple people and you need places for those other people to live and breathe, independent of each other.

Churchill famously painted, and was passably good at it. Less famously, he would retreat from his black dog moods by bricklaying. The red-brick wall that today runs around what was his former home at Chartwell he laid himself. Even in the darkest days of the war he would build walls, solitary and pensive, clearing his mind, refreshing his thoughts, recharging his batteries.

Nobody, certainly no book, can tell you how to nurture the 'other yous' – the bits that aren't the leader – but a book can tell you it matters and that you must. The leader-you can only thrive if the other yous are given a chance as well.

Use teamship rules to build healthy and happy teams

You can't climb mountains if you're not fit to do so and you can't expect your team to get behind you if they're always worrying about who's picking up the kids from school.

This is the final big myth of the leadership industry – it forgets it's all about real people's lives. And everybody's life is as complicated as your own. Everyone is dealing with their own shit. You've got to understand that before you can get people to follow you. If the spirit is willing, but the practicalities get in the way – it's never going to work. Inspirational speeches don't look after sick kids. Today's No Bullshit Leader must create human-scale solutions – not just enterprise-scale solutions. People aren't machines; they get tired, ill, bored and disillusioned.

The leader has a practical and moral obligation to create environments that work for the people who work within them. Who wants to run a 'team' whose breaks are monitored, who don't get to go outside without permission, whose opportunities extend to not getting fired, who are simply drones? I don't. If you've read this far

– neither do you. Great teams set their own rules based around the delivery of the objective. And their own rules are those that work for the members of the team, not the HR department.

Sir Clive Woodward talks of creating teamship rules within his teams. These are behavioural rules agreed by the team themselves (and approved by the leader) which define how they choose to work together and how they will hold each other to account. For example, on time-keeping and social media use. It's an easy idea to copy.

Tomorrow, your team should meet and agree together what teamship rules (or simple everyday behaviours) they will adopt to allow them all to be as effective and as efficient as possible, and at the same time find ways to work together that suit their real lives. For example:

- Perhaps some are morning people who want to start early but not finish late, with others the opposite.

- Everyone always moans about timekeeping – so agree collective rules to fix it. For example, agree to work to Lombardi Time. (Vince Lombardi is one of the most iconic sports coaches in US history. He expected his team to always be fifteen minutes early, to be 'on time' was to be late – hence Lombardi Time.)

- Everybody always complains about meetings – too many and too long. Decide how you want to fix this – the answer is up to the team and the team then owns it.

- What if a team member's child or partner is ill – how can you create teamship rules that help?

- If you've finished for the day make it mandatory to go home – kill presentee-ism.

Some might find these trivial, others idealistic, but I've run similar exercises many times, and they are easy, liberating and make an enormous impact on people's lives. It is amazing how often apparently small but intractable barriers cause difficulties for people that in turn have a disproportionate impact on their effectiveness, happiness, focus or health. In my experience, the possibilities of the exercise are almost endless. When asked to do so, teams strive to set realistic, healthy and respectful behaviours for themselves – which create micro-cultures that bend to suit the varied needs of everybody in the team. And, ultimately, cultures that deliver. Remember, a great culture is one that allows your team to outperform.

Teams that think this way are better teams – they focus on the real-life problems that get in the way of them being as effective as possible. If you're a morning person work in the morning. If an evening person, the evening. Teamship works when the team agrees the principles within the context of delivering better results. If the results don't come, this is a classic two-way door: just revert back. The principle is not that 'every idea is a good idea', but rather that you encourage the team to figure out how they work in ways that work for them. With a little imagination and ambition you'll be surprised how flexible you can be.

Take care of yourself physically and emotionally

Finally we come to the most basic building blocks of all: your mental and physical health. The leader must manage their own well-being, and they must also look out for the well-being of their team. Healthy organisations look out for each other and have support systems (both formal and informal) to help people when they need it – and we all need them sometimes. You ignore these for yourself at your peril.

As the leader, you have to look after yourself. If you don't, how good are you going to be at creating a culture that works for others? If you don't find spaces to recharge, refresh, keep fit, learn and laugh, is your team going to? We each must find our own answers to ensure we exercise in whatever way we enjoy, that we pay attention to, and find balance in what we eat and drink, that we find time and space to switch off and ask for help if we need it. Our health is the most basic building block upon which all else depends, and the most important influence on that is the simple common-sense choices we make every day.

That's all this book is about. It's about having a clear idea what it is you're trying to do and a clear plan for how to do it. It's about making sure you're focusing on the right stuff and learning from your mistakes. Your own mental and physical health are things you need to think about, for yourself and in order to be a long-term effective leader.

Not long after I first became a CEO I took my team for a two-day away day on a course called the Energy Project. The core idea of the programme was that when people feel at their best – spiritually, emotionally, mentally and physically – they focus more deeply, think more creatively, make better decisions and lead more effectively. It was a great course. It taught me that in order to lead (or succeed) in any organisation, you need to consider all of the different facets of who you are.

We sweated every morning, we measured our body fat, we studied nutrition, we considered how our energy levels fluctuated through the week and through each day, we discussed how our behaviours affected others and how their behaviours affected us. We meditated, looked into our souls, wrote letters of gratitude to people we never usually thanked and finished by writing personal action plans.

None of it was about our day jobs. None of it was about our skills. All of it was about how we make ourselves fit to lead and how our actions improve or worsen the mental and spiritual well-being of those we work with. It made me consider for the first time the richness and complexity of teams. Up to that point I had relied on hard work and smarts – after the Energy Project I felt I had gone from seeing in monochrome to seeing in multicolour. In some ways it was the beginning of my leadership journey.

You don't need to go on a training programme to get to grips with these questions – in reality you know it already. You just need to begin to do it. I'm not one to preach, but you know it's true.

We all tell ourselves stories about why we can't do these things. 'I hate the gym' or 'I don't have time' or 'I could never give up chocolate'. But this is a book about leadership, not an exercise plan. You don't have to go to the gym, you don't have to give anything up, you don't need lots of time. You just need to find your balance and your way. I don't buy that you can't – and neither, deep down, do you.

In his book *UnF*ck Yourself*, Gary John Bishop reframes 'can' and 'can't' as willing and unwilling. 'Before you say you can,' he writes, 'you have to ask yourself the question, "am I willing?"'. Conversely, he argues, unwillingness can also prove as powerful a motivator to action. 'Only when you're unwilling to put up with the bullshit any longer will you pick up the shovel and start digging ... Once you frame the obstacles in your life as a matter of willing and unwilling ... you can break through the self-imposed barriers.'

The question is, are you unwilling to simply go on as you are? Are you willing to find a way to health and balance? Are you unwilling to keep grinding through without a plan? Are you willing to allow 'being too busy at work' to get in the way of your health?

This isn't about being a corporate athlete (what a horrendous phrase that truly is) or a midlife triathlete, but make sure you look after yourself, your physical health, your mental health, your spiritual health – and do the same for your team. Of course, it's none of your business whether your team eat healthily, or indeed, how they spend their lives outside of work, but you can create a culture that allows their various lives to coexist.

Unless of course you lead a sports team, in which case you probably need to make sure they can run a bit as well.

EVEN LESS BULLSH*T

7

LEADING YOURSELF

The successful leader must be a selfish leader: to be consistently effective she must take as much care of herself as she does of others.

For a culture to be healthy it needs to recover from the busy times through downtime – when you get up, walk away and go home.

Learn from the Stoics – your emotions are detached from external events and therefore fully within your control:

Choose not to be harmed – and you won't feel harmed. Don't feel harmed – and you haven't been.

Your feelings and emotions do not in any way affect the fundamental skill base of your team. Learn to trust your process.

⇩

Accept the inevitability of self-doubt. I'm Chris Hirst and I'm an insecure leader.

⇩

Don't be afraid to be vulnerable. It's not a sign of weakness, it's a proof of strength, and without it nothing gets done.

⇩

Live a whole life – leadership is only one part of our complicated lives. The leader-you can only thrive if the other-yous are given a chance as well.

⇩

Use teamship rules to build healthy and happy teams.

⇩

Take care of yourself physically and emotionally.

LEADING CHANGE

Unless someone like you cares a whole awful lot,
nothing is going to get better. It's not.

– Dr Seuss

CHANGE MANAGEMENT IS A massive topic. We have
already established that all leadership is about change,
but sometimes you find yourself leading an organisation that is truly broken or lost, full of directionless and
demoralised people. It might be a Sunday league team
or a major corporation. The scale differs, but the human
symptoms are the same. For all leaders it's the ultimate
challenge – a truly daunting experience. If all leadership
is hill-climbing, this is Mount Everest.

And never has the need to master this challenge been
more pressing. We live in a world of unprecedented
disruption. Our high streets are being ravaged by a former
online bookstore; Hollywood's biggest threat began life
as a DVD rental company. From the way we eat and shop
to how we learn and travel, transformational change has
become the norm.

Of course, with change comes opportunity, and for this reason, organisational change is a well-studied subject – a favourite of business schools. There are some good and useful books on the subject (I can recommend John Kotter, for example), but as with much else to do with leadership, there is a whole lot of bullshit as well. And even amongst the non-bullshit, much that is written and taught falls into idealistic theory, leaving the reader scratching her head and asking herself, yes, but what should I actually do?

It's a good time, therefore, to return to my earlier equation:

Leadership Impact = (objectives + strategy + team + values + motivation) x (action)

Leading change is defined by action. Yes, of course strategy remains critical, and in a disorienting world your future direction may be difficult to determine, but take heart from the knowledge that it is just as unclear for everyone else. Nobody can see the future. Everyone is building on what feels like shifting sands. But the danger this poses the leader is that the greater their uncertainty the greater their inertia. They become like a pilot at the end of a runway waiting for the clouds to lift so they can take off. Unfortunately for today's leaders the fog isn't going to lift – which means that to take off you must learn to fly even when the weather is bad.

I have over a decade of practical experience transforming broken businesses into world-beaters, and I can tell you that it is possible to take off in even the thickest fog. It's difficult, and there will be many bumps (to put it mildly) along the way, but with a clear mind and a clear plan you can do it.

I have outlined in the following pages my ten key steps for designing and executing your organisation's transformation programme – whether it be ten people or 10,000. The watchwords for the No Bullshit Leader are, keep it simple and be ambitious. It is critical that your team believe that you, as the leader, know where you're going and, of course, that they know too.

No organisation is a lost cause. Here are my ten key steps to make sure yours is on the winning side.

1. Look, listen and learn – or, The Reception Test

Define in as simple and clear a manner as possible the position, status or performance of your team today.

There are many possible solutions to this task: it could include financial information, position in a league table, customer satisfaction or data on the performance of the market, the economy as a whole or that of your competitors. It must also include qualitative measures, such as the environment, culture (of course), the quality and appropriateness of the people – and their mood. You should meet with clients, customers and staff, visit customers who have recently stopped working with you, read exit interviews, go to the pub, buy drinks and listen.

This stage involves a lot of listening.

This is of course all pretty obvious stuff. What you must also do however is trust your gut. Listening and researching is very important, and provides evidence around which you can begin to build a thesis; it reassures yourself and others that you've done your homework. But, it's also useful here to revisit Colin Powell's 40/70 rule:

> *Don't take action if you have only enough information to give you a less than 40 per cent chance of being right, but if you have waited until you're more than 70 per cent certain then you have waited too long.*

Powell's doctrine urges action. It reminds us that hard facts are only part of the information-gathering process. The other lesson from the 40/70 rule is to remember your gut instinct. What does your gut tell you?

A great example involves what I call the Reception Test.

Several years ago I took over as CEO of a business that at the time comprised around ten similar-sized units, most of which were located at different sites around central London. These businesses, though all in the same industry, operated in distinct and separate parts of the sector. Some were high-performing, while others were broken. I rapidly discovered that I could tell how an individual unit was performing, and hence how it felt about itself, by simply standing in its reception. This sounds ridiculous, but it was true.

It is an almost trivial observation, but one which hides a wider truth. In the same way that body language can unknowingly give away what people are really feeling, the same can apply to a team or even an entire organisation. A team's body language, its subtle signs and signals, can show you how it really feels about itself and how it is doing.

Try it tomorrow with your team. What is its body language and do you like what it's saying? How does it portray itself on its website and as you walk through the front door? What are the first words and images it uses: how are people dressed; do they smile and make eye contact; are meeting rooms left tidy or not; are the posters on the wall recent or out of date ... I could go on.

Every team can change its body language and can do it very quickly. Sometimes it is enough to simply point it out, like asking somebody you're talking to to uncross their arms.

Have you ever walked into a house and wondered why the owners never quite finished painting a particular wall, or got round to fixing the broken skirting board? The last 5 per cent can be the difference between a beautiful room and one that looks half finished or even unloved. Over time these last little jobs just got pushed back further, to be done on a 'tomorrow' that never quite came. I'm sure we can all think of examples in our own houses. Eventually, familiarity blinds us to these small imperfections: we know they're there, and we have it in our heads that one day we'll fix them, but over time we come to see the room as we'd *like* it to be, rather than how it really is. When people come to your house it is these unfinished corners that you long ago stopped noticing that leap out to them. It's only when we walk into the room as a newcomer that we see it as it really is.

It's the same when outsiders walk into your

organisation or meet your team. What do their fresh eyes see that yours don't?

Challenge yourself, whether it's your tenth day or your tenth year, to walk in tomorrow and look around afresh. You'll be amazed what you see if you really look. Why hasn't anyone replaced the dead plant in the corner of reception, or peeled the yellowing Sellotape off the meeting room walls? Why hasn't anyone cleaned the changing room, or repainted the lines in the car park? Once you see with fresh eyes you will spot flaws everywhere – often easy flaws to fix, if only somebody would just take the time to do it. And once you're aware of them, trust me, they gnaw at you until they're done.

Of course, as a corollary, the good news is that it is possible to alter aspects of your team's body language, and therefore begin the process of actually changing the team itself, by making quick and easy changes to what are ostensibly relatively simple and cosmetic matters. If the crappy businesses had crappy receptions, perhaps simply sorting out the reception area could make the unit a little better. Just tidying up can make the organisation feel different about itself. Change can begin by simply tidying up reception. Sounds ridiculous? Trust me, it's true.

When you feel you know enough, resist the temptation to dress up what you find in flowery language and management speak. Nine times out of ten, you will have 'discovered' the glaringly obvious. However, remember, in many teams and organisations the glaringly obvious is hidden in plain sight. Your first task is to have the courage and the confidence to state the bleeding obvious. You'll be surprised how many people thank you for it: cut to it, say it as it is, don't bullshit.

Your first big leadership challenge, then, is not for you to identify the problem (as we've established, that's not usually that difficult), but for you to ensure the rest of the organisation both understands the problem and shares, however uncomfortably, an appreciation of the need for change. It is impossible for a team to change if it doesn't want to. Like curing an addiction, you can only begin once you've acknowledged you've got a problem. Change begins with a collective desire to move from where you are today.

2. Define your objective and find your 'first five'

You can't do it on your own – who are your 'first five'?*
(*It doesn't have to be five.)

If you have done a good job of convincing your team of the need to change, then the task of getting them to buy into a positive and clearly expressed future is not usually that difficult.

Here it is critical that you create a coalition to help define the objective, to own it along with you and crucially become the shock troops to begin to make it happen. If you try and make do you will likely fail. This core team may comprise people who are already in place, or they may be people you bring in, but most commonly they will be a mix of both. Primarily you must be absolutely sure of their technical ability, and that they are 100 per cent committed to the team and your project.

Nina Steeples, Deputy Headteacher of Springfield Primary School in East London, talks of the 'first five' when they came together to fix what had been a perennial problem school. On joining the school, the new headteacher brought in her A-team of four like-minded deputies, of which Steeples was one. Together they agreed their immediate next steps, the long-term objective and how they were going to get there.

A change leader needs to rapidly identify their core team, either from inside or outside the organisation. In their case, Steeples continues, they did three things in common: divided the key tasks equally between them, set the example they wanted others to follow through their actions (they all remained in hands-on teaching roles) and – as with change leaders everywhere – worked very hard. It's worth noting that for them defining their objective was relatively straightforward. They didn't overthink it. They wanted to create a great school out of the broken one they had inherited. Their energies were spent working out how.

Consider your core team as part of an ink-dot strategy. As dots of ink dripped on blotting paper spread slowly until they meet, so should your 'first five' focus on gradually changing the culture, behaviours and skills (and, if necessary, composition) of the rest of the organisation. Gradually this small core team expands to a wider and wider coalition – the faster it does so, the faster you'll progress.

Most organisations are aware, without much effort on your behalf, of the challenges they face. Take for example the demise of the once mighty Kodak – they could see what was coming; the problem was, they couldn't work out what to do about it. This is a common problem. Many failing teams don't believe that change is possible – even if there is a general consensus that it would be desirable. This is exacerbated in situations where previous management has come and gone (accompanied by much fanfare and ambitious promises) without discernible improvement. You, as the new leader, are just seen as the next schmuck doomed to try and fail while everyone else has learned to keep their heads down and wait for you to pass.

Rather than convincing people of the merit of their ambition, the key challenge for the leader in this situation is to make people believe that its *attainment* is possible. The theory, they might think, is great, but how on earth are we ever going to get from here to there? (For those who have been paying attention, that is the leader's job, and why we're all here.)

Twice now I've stood in front of broken businesses that had been expending all their energy just to keep their heads above water and told them that quite simply our ambition was to be the best. Not better. Best. We spent little more time than that defining our ambition. Saying it was easy; making everybody (and from time to time myself) believe that it was possible was the real challenge.

Therefore, at this stage you need to achieve three things of equal importance:

1. Find your 'first five'.* (*It doesn't have to be five – I'll leave that to you to decide.)

2. Define your objective, which must be expressed simply and concisely in terms you and all your partners, employees and customers can easily understand (see Chapter 2: Leading to Where?).

3. Make your team or organisation believe that change (in the first instance, frankly, any change) is possible.

3. Break free and create belief

Create fast, visible change to prove that it is possible (and therefore build belief and confidence in your team).

Change is a physical activity, but it is a physical activity often derailed by a whole array of psychological and emotional factors, the most significant of which is not your team's unwillingness to change but rather their belief that change can't happen to them. Your job is to inspire the belief that change can happen, that it's going to happen and that you are the person who is going to lead it.

Here therefore, I suggest a possible rewrite to the Leadership Impact equation (Chaper 2). For the No Bullshit Leader of change it becomes:

Change = (objectives + strategy + team + values + motivation) x (action)^2

To steal someone else's phrase – to fix a broken team you must move fast and break stuff. Leadership Impact is biased towards action, and in the early stages of your project you should behave as though it's action squared.

Change is usually portrayed as a linear process, with a start, a middle and an end. For simplicity and clarity I have portrayed it this way myself elsewhere in this book. This model is useful up to a point, but in reality it doesn't work like that at all. Real change is lumpy and bumpy, and your next most pressing task (more important than all the sensible stuff like starting points and visions) is convincing the team that change for them is not just desirable, but doable.

Rather than it being linear, think of your journey as being in the shape of a cone, with your starting point at the centre of the base, where there is a post driven hard into the ground. Your final destination, as defined by your ambition, is the tip. As complicated and intimidating (if not more than a little overwhelming) as this all is, to make matters worse you cannot even begin your journey until you have removed the post from the ground. This is your beginning on day 1.

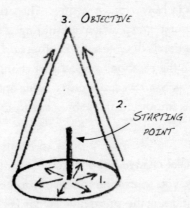

1. Firstly you must free yourself from the post driven into the ground. Direction is less important than moving as far from the starting point as fast as possible.

Here you are, stuck at point (1), your end point (3) seeming an impossibly long way away, and everybody around you is standing, arms folded, waiting to see what you – the most recent of a long line – can do.

Imagine that your organisation is tethered to this post that has been hammered hard into the ground; in order to begin to change you must first free yourselves. To do so you throw your weight against it first from one direction and then the other; you pull, push, scream, kick and shout. It's hard work to get it out, and frankly you couldn't care less what you do in order to wrench it out. When you're covered in sweat and up to your knees in mud, what matters isn't some lofty final goal; what matters is that only once you're free can you really begin. In reality many leaders and many organisations never manage to get the bloody post out of the ground.

This is how change begins. The crucial insight the leader must grasp when rebuilding a broken team or organisation is that initially the direction of travel matters less than the creation of belief that change is possible. At this stage, your destination is sufficiently distant to be way less important than the need to create energy and belief.

First, you establish a need to change and then you must make change happen very quickly. You warm the muscles, you smash the concrete, you make Monday feel different from the preceding Friday. Be iconoclastic, be fearless; change as much as you dare as quickly as you can. (These topics are covered in more detail in Chapters 3 and 4.) You'll be amazed at the energy you liberate. And if some of the stuff you try doesn't work or doesn't help then simply reverse it.

Never be afraid to be wrong – in fact, embrace it. Be afraid of inaction.

'Freeing the post' is a critical first step in change. It makes your organisation believe that change is possible, and that change can happen to them. And crucially it begins the process of making them believe in you. It proves you're different, that you're not just another leader who is full of talk and empty on action. Your first objective is to move the company as far away from its starting point as quickly as possible, more like concentric circles in a pond than a straight line.

4. Make the objective personal – for everybody

Ensure your team understand why change is in their personal interest (and do the same for all other stakeholders – for example, customers or parents).

It is often said that people don't like change. In my experience this is often not the case. That said, many leaders make the mistake of forgetting that their team is actually a collection of disparate individuals, brought together by the chance of the recruiting process.

Smart people in a broken organisation will often take little persuading that change is necessary, while at the same time being very uncomfortable, if not actively resistant, to it for their own personal reasons.

A leader must therefore do more than simply help people understand why it is in the best interests of the *whole* to change. They must make them understand that change is also in their *individual* and personal interests.

Ultimately, if there are people who never buy in then it is in both their and your interests that they go elsewhere. Organisational change is not an abstract event that happens to homogeneous groups; rather it comes from individuals who decide or are persuaded that it is in their best interests for them to approach often familiar tasks in a different way.

When speaking of change as a leader you must be careful that your audience doesn't think, 'Yes, he's right, if only everybody else would change.' What you want is for them to spend very little time thinking about all the things everybody else could do better, and instead to think only of the things that they themselves need to do differently.

The way to achieve this is for you to help them understand the eventual benefits for them personally, even if the process is uncomfortable or difficult in the short-term. Too often change is presented as a painful process that is necessary for the organisation as a whole, but with no explanation as to why it is also great news for the individuals within it.

The same approach should be taken with all stakeholders (for example, parents or customers). Customers are often told that change is necessary without being told what's in it for them. There are many great (in a bad way) examples of this in my own industry. New leadership teams arrive and grandly announce that everything that went before was crap. There are numerous cases of large clients hearing this and deciding that since the new leadership feels that what they have been paying handsomely for was now considered rubbish, they would take their custom elsewhere. It's so unnecessary and avoidable, yet it happens all the time.

A leader must keep in mind the various ambitions and perspectives of their stakeholders, for example employees and customers, and frame why change is in their interests. This should be done explicitly, clearly and regularly: people have short memories, particularly at times of pressure and stress. The additional benefit is that people are far more prepared to tolerate short-term discomfort if they are convinced that at the end of the process there is a clear benefit to them. It's not difficult, it just so often gets forgotten.

The leader must craft their messaging to each constituency and stick at it. They must carefully explain why change is in everyone's interest and connect the actions they are taking to the vision and strategy they describe.

5. Tell it how it is and hear it as it is

Be honest with yourself and others – and create a culture where your team can speak truth to power.

All leaders, and especially leaders of change, must accept that they will be forced to confront, and often publicly state, uncomfortable truths. Leaders often choose the complicated language of business consultants to obscure these or, lacking in confidence, to demonstrate their intellectual prowess. Resist this temptation.

In Chapter 4, we discussed the dependent cultures that 'Caesars' create. Instead, an effective leader must build an adult-to-adult relationship with their team, something that can be difficult and requires time, patience and hard work to achieve. When it works, every member of the team knows their role and the roles of others, and there exists a mutual trust between them. This is the secret power of the Nordstrom Rule Book (page 60) – and indeed to the changes Timpson made (page 61). They had the effect of creating high-trust environments.

Trust requires honesty and consistency. A leader can only lead if people are willing to follow. Many leaders mistake popularity with trust. It is not necessary for a leader to be liked. What is crucial is that the leader trusts their team and in turn is trusted by them.

A leader's job is not to be popular. It is to make the collective of individuals in her team more effective. They should not be rude, undiplomatic or disrespectful, but clear, direct and consistent. Your team must know that you're for real.

You must also understand that honesty is a two-way process. A leader who 'tells it how it is' but is completely unwilling to accept or hear criticism is as bad (or worse) than the opposite. The leader's behaviour should reflect the culture they need to create – and an effective culture is one where everybody, from the top down, are able to have the right conversations. And for the right conversations to happen it is a fundamental requirement that all are able to speak truth to power.

As a leader you don't need to have all the answers

– and indeed, nor will you. You won't have all the best
ideas; you won't always be right. You need to ensure that
the right conversations are had and that the quality of an
individual's contribution is uncorrelated to their seniority.
For it to be true that great ideas can come from anywhere,
you need to make it happen through your actions.

Sir Maurice Oldfield, the legendary former head of
MI6 on whom it is rumoured John le Carré modelled
George Smiley, once said of his relationship with the then
Prime Minister Margaret Thatcher, that it was his job to
tell her what she didn't want to hear. You need to make
sure you're being told the things you don't want to hear.
They're way more important than the honeyed words
some may choose to drip in your ear.

Having the 'right' conversation can sometimes be
emotionally difficult, intimidating and even scary. In
these instances it can feel easier to avoid them. Bright,
motivated people can be passionate about their views
– and passions can easily become arguments. You don't
want a team who spend their lives shouting at each other,
but it's important that the right conversations are had.
An effective culture is not one that doesn't row, but one
where people are able to row without falling out. The
secret is building mutual trust and respect. As long as
people don't feel that their values or they themselves are
being attacked, they can argue – find common ground, or
agree to disagree – then perfectly happily move on. Good
teams are passionate. Bad teams bottle things up. Getting
stuff out in the open, done correctly, is actually the best
way to maintain harmony. Unspoken disagreements

fester and lead to politics, resentment and mistrust.

We have established already that one of the leader's most important challenges is to get people to believe in your vision. You can't achieve this if they think you're a bullshitter. It's as simple as that. They don't have to like you, but they have to believe you. If they believe you and you believe in yourself, you have a chance.

You need to tell it as it is, but you must also be prepared to hear it as it is. Creating a culture of honesty is the leader's secret sauce. Without honesty there can be no trust. Without trust, no progress.

6. *Schwerpunkt:* the point of maximum effort

Define the single point of focus that will most effectively move you towards your ultimate objective – and commit to it fully.

During the Napoleonic Wars of the nineteenth century a Prussian general, Carl von Clausewitz, wrote *On War*, one of the most influential strategy books of all time. In it he gave us his most famous quote, 'War is the continuation of politics by other means'.

Clausewitz also introduced the strategic concept of *schwerpunkt*, which roughly translates as 'key point'. He used it to mean a strategic objective or focus of effort directed at the weakest point. *Schwerpunkt* tells us that in any situation there are any number of important tasks, but one is disproportionately important in achieving your goals.

For example, a new leader takes over an under-performing unit with an ambitious remit for dramatic change and is readily able to get a handle on the issues. You quickly describe a clear and motivating picture of the future – 'We are going to be the most admired low-cost airline in the world. Not simply better, we are going to be the best' – and be able to connect that future to the motivations and aspirations of a large majority of your team.

As is always the case, however, it is evident to you and your 'first five' that reaching your goal will require a significant and wide-ranging improvement in performance across the organisation, both quantitative and qualitative. You must therefore decide where to begin, ensuring that the whole organisation is clear on the location of the point of maximum effort and their part in that effort. This is your *schwerpunkt*, a simple expression of the team's point of maximum effort.

Examples might be:

We will pitch and win more new accounts than any of our competitors; we will become the best company in the country at pitching.

Or

We will make the best coffee in London, by learning to roast and grind our own.

Or

Our customer waiting times will be the shortest in the market.

Or

Our customer satisfaction will be 10 per cent higher over the next twelve months.

These are not necessarily your ultimate objectives, but are clearly defined points of strategic focus that will most rapidly get you to it.

The whole team must be clear and focused on the *schwerpunkt*. If well chosen, its clarity is liberating. It has the obvious consequence of identifying the areas of greatest priority, but also, by direct implication, those that are not; it helps you decide what you should do, but just as importantly, it tells you what not to do. This does not mean that other areas should never be addressed, but rather that they should be addressed in a clear priority order.

So if scoring goals is the team's greatest challenge, single-mindedly fix it. Once you've made improvement here there may be other aspects of the team's play that have suffered, or that become the new priorities; move to these next. If 'making London's greatest coffee' is the objective, then staff training isn't the *schwerpunkt*, except where it links directly to this objective: the rebranding is important, but not yet.

In all teams there are always things that need fixing. High-performing and clever people (which you are) are very good at spotting stuff that doesn't work. The challenge the leader faces is that these things cannot all be of equal importance in striving for your ultimate goal.

Your *schwerpunkt* is your team's overriding point of focus. It is task one, two and three. Don't fudge it or hide it – commit to it fully.

Ask yourself, what is the top-down task that will most effectively unlock your team's route towards your stated objective.

7. Prioritising means deciding what to stop doing

Focus on what you should be doing (to be most effective), not what leadership books and orthodoxy tell you you ought to be doing.

Warren Buffett, on-and-off the world's richest man, once asked his pilot what his ambitions were – surely he aspired to more than simply flying him from A to B? His pilot admitted that this was true. Buffett then asked him to write down his ambitions list, with the greatest and most significant at the top. Once he'd completed this, Buffett took a pen and struck off everything except for that in the No. 1 spot. His advice: the only way you really achieve your greatest ambitions is by ruthlessly removing or stopping pursuing everything else. The greatest successes are achieved not by defining what it is you most want, but by identifying all those other secondary things that distract and dilute your effort and then stopping doing these altogether.

The lesson: success as a leader is as dependent on what you stop doing as it is what you start.

For many leaders reading this, the ultimate measure of success will be numeric, be it points gained, money made or exams passed. Whatever it is for you, today there are many additional pressures on a leader that can obscure this clarity. We live in a world of HR programmes, security audits, timesheets, hiring guidelines and disciplinary policies; cultures, values, emails, speaker engagements, marketing, PR and social media, CSR programmes and offsites. All these things and many more crowd into a leader's day. It is very easy for what had seemed clear to become muddied and lost in the maelstrom.

Furthermore, it is easy in any organisation to see how many of these activities can be improved, and all seem to cry out for attention. In your round of listening, different parts of the organisation will accurately and eloquently identify the weaknesses and room for improvement in one or many of these areas: our profile is too low; staff engagement could be improved; the culture isn't clear; nobody can remember the values; client retention is poor, etc. You too, right now, will be able to identify many aspects of your organisation that are crying out for a little TLC (if you can't, you're not looking hard enough).

The No Bullshit Change Leader must learn to listen, but also filter. She must know the state of the business, and be ruthlessly single-minded in identifying not just where to start, but what to ignore. For now. The alternative is a classic pitfall of those attempting to lead change.

In my first management role I was part of a team that experienced six years of trying and failing. During these dark years, this is the mistake we made, again and again. We improved the peripheries: we hired some better people, we had a better CSR programme, we had better training programmes and better marketing, but the business moved hardly an inch against the metrics that really mattered.

This is a common mistake. It's what I call the bottom-up approach: the attempt to diligently fix all the visible problems in the expectation that as you do they will gradually lift the organisation, as pumping out water lifts a sinking ship. The problem is, in practice it doesn't work.

Another way of looking at it is that leadership teams spend way too much of their time doing the things they think they *ought* to be doing, the kind of things that traditional leadership books tell you to do. My advice: don't do the things you think you *ought* to be doing. Do the things that your objectives and *schwerpunkt* tell you that you *should* be doing – those that will contribute most directly and most immediately to your No. 1 ambition. Take Buffett's advice and stop doing everything else.

Essentially, if you want to run a great team, it will need to be great at many different things – the big and the small. However, you must tackle them in the order your objectives dictate to be the most important, not bottom-up and certainly not all at once (see the Eisenhower Matrix on page 39).

8. Relentless, continuous improvement

Change doesn't happen in great leaps, but is the continual search for marginal improvements. You must ruthlessly hunt them down.

In the kitchens of high-end restaurants they talk of *mise en place*, literally 'putting in place'. It refers to the preparation of the kitchen: the organising and arranging of the ingredients, equipment and space prior to beginning cooking. It's the bit you don't see on TV before Gordon Ramsay starts swearing.

At this stage you have completed the *mise en place* (you

may have already done a little swearing), and now you must begin to cook.

To return to the cone diagram from earlier: having dragged the post from the ground, you now find yourself somewhere on the outer edge of the base. The direction of travel toward your objective shown at its tip (point 3) now becomes your priority. This process will be a series of actions, big and small, that fit within the narrative you have described. These must be consistent with your *schwerpunkt*.

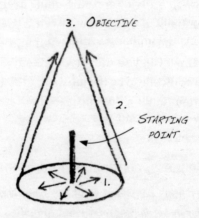

3. *OBJECTIVE*

2.

STARTING POINT

1.

1. *Firstly you must free yourself from the post driven into the ground. Direction is less important than moving as far from the starting point as fast as possible.*

2. *Once free, direction of travel becomes your priority*

Think of this as finding ways to make Monday feel different to the preceding Friday: what will be different next week, what we will do next to give us a different perspective, break old habits or enable better performance. This might be anything from a major new initiative to, more commonly, frequent, small actions. For example, it could be something like holding a familiar, regular leadership meeting at a different time or in a different place. You'll be surprised how effective small steps such as this can be at getting people to think and behave differently.

There is clear logic to this approach. Very often the challenges and problems you and your teams face are familiar; the same questions reoccur. The challenge for the leader is therefore not in finding the solution to a completely new question, but rather the need to find new solutions to familiar questions (for example: How do we maintain our margins with our largest customers?). You may not be able to change the questions, but you can change the context in which they are considered. Every tiny step helps, and you'll be surprised at the power of environment and context to help you find fresh answers.

Whatever it is, the leader needs to stop the concrete from resetting until they are sure they are well on the way toward their eventual goal. To achieve this they must focus hard on maintaining the momentum of change.

This is a variation on Dave Brailsford's principle: the aggregation of marginal gains. Brailsford was Director of Sport for the GB Olympic Cycling Team during a time when the team went from nobodies to world champions. He then moved on to a similar role at Team Sky, where they came to dominate road cycling – most notably the Tour de France. If you aren't familiar with it, 'marginal gains' is a simple and powerful concept. It says that improvements in team performance are achieved not in huge leaps and bounds, but in the steady, gradual, deliberate accumulation of small or even tiny improvements in pursuit of a clear and universally understood goal. In it we can see echoes of Professor Chambliss's conclusions (Chapter 6: The mundanity of excellence).

So ingrained in the Team Sky culture did it become, that for a period Brailsford even employed a Director of Marginal Gains to hunt out every possible micro-improvement. These myriad tiny changes, however, led to radical innovations that overturned nearly a century of received wisdom on track and road racing, and made Sky into one of the most successful teams in world sport. Bike frames were reinvented, skinsuits, goggles and helmets redesigned; riding positions were studied in wind tunnels; diet and supplements were individualised; a team psychologist was hired to build mental strength and stamina; the team bus was reimagined around the athletic needs of the riders; warm-up and warm-down zones were introduced (and rapidly copied); individual mattresses and pillows were even transported from hotel to hotel to ensure riders slept in the same bed every night (or as near as possible).

The principle of marginal gains did not simply aim to train the riders better or improve the bikes, it considered every aspect of a cycle team's life and existence. Brailsford saw that excellence required a continuous search for small improvements, each one imagined, tested, tried and then either accepted or rejected. Its brilliance lies in its persistence, its acknowledgement of the continuous nature of change and the holistic nature of its vision. This is its greatest revolution, rather than simply its granularity.

Right now, with a little effort, you will be able to think of a whole array of individually small steps your team could make that would make you collectively more effective and your environment more conducive to improvement. You may dismiss some as too trivial to count, but it is exactly the accumulation of these tiny steps that over time builds noticeable improvement. So for example consider the physical experience of visitors (especially new customers) when they arrive at a business. It's a simple, everyday event that has some equivalence in many areas of life, and indeed something we have all done at some point.

So, for example:

- Can the visibility and useablity of the contact section of the website be improved? Is there a map that links to Google Maps?

- Is there advice on parking and transport links?

- Is the office clearly signed and visible for a new visitor?

- What is the external first impression of the building?

- What is the first impression when you walk in, and is it what the organisation would desire?

- Who is the first person that a visitor speaks to and what is this experience like?

- How easy is it to find (or be directed to) where a visitor wants to go after arriving?

- What is the experience of waiting in reception?
- How long typically do people have to wait?
- What is the experience of going from reception to a meeting room?

This is a familiar experience to us all, and I could have been much more granular. I guarantee that if you put your mind to it you will be able to dramatically improve each step of this customer experience, and you'll be able to do a lot of it without spending much (if any) money. Now imagine any number of other everyday parts of how your organisation operates and take a similar approach. This is marginal gains.

9. Be consistent

A consistent narrative gives understanding and context to the multitude of actions you and the team must undertake. Words, actions and totems must dovetail to create a consistent whole.

A leader must be consistent. From the smallest teams to whole organisations undergoing massive and rapid upheaval, it is important to remember that for many people the majority of their day job will be much the same, most of the time (at least initially). Much of change is about breaking these routines, finding ways to see the familiar with fresh eyes and finding new answers or approaches to common tasks. This is why the steps I have outlined thus far are so important, and why it is so difficult (but important) to smash the concrete.

I recently shared a beer with a very successful rock

musician, a man who has what many would consider a dream job, touring the world playing his music in front of thousands. Even he, however, found himself battling against the tyranny of routine, and how it can severely undermine both the enjoyment of an incredible job and the creative process. As a group, they found they had to continually ensure they didn't let the exceptional become mundane, or even irritating. If touring the globe with a rock band can become routine anything can – if you let it.

Achieving and sustaining a change programme requires that you continuously challenge familiar routines and ensure you are cutting through. If somebody is having a terrible day because a client has been yelling at them for most of it, your carefully crafted email explaining the new corporate culture and values isn't likely to make much impression.

That's why it's critical that your words are consistent, memorable and impactful, that you focus very clearly on a small number of messages and ensure they stick through repeating them ad nauseam. This creates context and understanding for actions you take; even the most inspired decision, without context, can appear arbitrary. You may quickly become bored of hearing yourself, but the majority will take much longer to reach that point.

Your objective is that your words and actions dovetail to create a coherent whole in the minds of your team.

■ Consistency of language re-enforces your ambition and your description of the change-journey the team is undertaking.

- Actions, big and small, push the team forward, but need to be given context by your words.

- Totems are a daily reminder of both your destination and journey, and intrude physically into people's daily routines.

10. Prepare yourself for the long haul

Change leadership is a marathon in reverse: begin fast, but prepare yourself for a long and bumpy ride.

Whereas in a 1,500m race the pace is steady and accelerates into a lung-bursting, leg-destroying sprint over the last 200m, leading change is like a marathon in reverse. You should go as quickly as you can at first while being realistic that such a pace may not be sustainable for the medium-term.

Many leaders get to this stage: they initially do a good and diligent job and, bursting with enthusiasm, achieve fast and focused progress toward their goal. The problem, however, is that many programmes fail to fulfil their initial promise as the leader and their team tire or become derailed. To lead change the leader must prepare well, begin fast and, at least as importantly, have the energy and drive to continue the momentum of the project over the long run.

Change takes time. New habits and cultures can be formed, but don't underestimate how easy it is for old ones to re-emerge, particularly at times of stress and pressure. In the same way that a good sports coach continually monitors the performance of her charge and changes their drills to avoid boredom, overfamiliarity and stagnation, so must you continually search for the new to maintain the momentum and energy of the programme.

Leading change is a continually evolving process that requires the less sexy skills of stamina, grit and humility as much as the ones business books love: charisma, intelligence and energy. It is only possible to survive on endorphins, adrenalin and caffeine for so long, eventually you will need to live a life of balance and find a way of working (for yourself and your team) that is sustainable in the long-term. The leader is at her most valuable and must be most engaged when things are tough. Therefore, when it's all working, go play tennis (or whatever floats your boat) to recharge – in the certain knowledge that that happy state won't last long.

Finally, let's return to Nina Steeples at Springfield Primary. Do not be seduced by this book or any other into seeing change as a linear process with stages that you tick off like milestones along a road. Despite having an excellent, aligned and motivated team with the authority to act as they saw fit, it took three years of hard and continual graft before Steeples and her colleagues began to see tangible outward results. There is no rule to determine how long success will take – every single situation is unique. However, Steeples' experience, in common with thousands of other leaders, is that effective change takes time to come to fruition. And in her case, three years was just the first flowering – it took several more years of successes and failures before they could really say they had arrived. The school, having been in permanent crisis, is now one of the best in London, and is used as a model of best practice. They have great results and excellent relationships with parents and students, and tellingly, it's a place where great teachers aspire to work. They have created an enduring and replicable culture of excellence.

Their experience is typical of successful change programmes, and is why you must plan and prepare yourself and your team for a long journey. In many cases, the arrival at the top of the mountain merely reveals further ranges on the horizon.

EVEN LESS BULLSH*T

8

LEADING CHANGE

1. Look, listen and learn – or, The Reception Test
Define in as simple and clear a manner as possible
the position, status or performance of your
team today.

2. Define your objective and find your 'first five'
You can't do it on your own – who are your 'first
five'?* (*It doesn't have to be five.)

3. Break free and create belief
Create fast, visible change to prove that it is possible
(and therefore build belief and confidence in
your team).

4. Make the objective personal – for everybody
Ensure your team understands why change is in
their personal interest (and do the same for all other
stakeholders – for example, customers or parents).

⇩

5. Tell it how it is and hear it as it is

Be honest with yourself and others – and create a culture where your team can speak truth to power.

⇩

6. *Schwerpunkt*: the point of maximum effort

Define the single point of focus that will most effectively move you towards your ultimate objective – and commit to it fully.

⇩

7. Prioritising means deciding what to stop doing

Focus on what you should be doing (to be most effective), not what leadership books and orthodoxy tell you that you ought to be doing.

⇩

8. Relentless, continuous improvement

Change doesn't happen in great leaps, but is the continual search for marginal improvements. You must ruthlessly hunt them down.

⇩

9. Be consistent

A consistent narrative gives understanding and context to the multitude of actions you and the team must undertake. Words, actions and totems must dovetail to create a consistent whole.

⇩

10. Prepare yourself for the long haul

Change leadership is a marathon in reverse: begin
fast, but prepare yourself for a long and bumpy ride.

CONCLUSION

Life moves pretty fast. If you don't stop and look around once in a while you could miss it.

Ferris Bueller, *Ferris Bueller's Day Off*

THE PREMISE OF THIS BOOK is simple yet ambitious. It aims to wipe away the bullshit that surrounds the subject of leadership and in doing so encourage the reader to think afresh about what leadership really is and what should matter most to the modern leader, providing a straightforward framework around which the reader can build. It aims to liberate and inspire through the demystification of an overdiscussed subject.

Leadership is difficult but not complicated, and I intend for this book to encourage and enable many more people to recognise the leader they are or could be. Leading is simply the navigation of a group from a starting point in the present to a clearly defined alternative state in the future. The leader must express their starting point in simple, easy-to-understand terms, and define an ambitious, clear destination. They must build an effective culture that enables their teams to outperform, and that people choose to be part of. Ultimately, when the talking stops, progress is achieved through fast, effective decision-making.

The democratisation of leadership – or more properly, the democratisation of the opportunity to lead – is this book's ultimate goal. We need more leaders at all levels and from all parts of our society. The idea of a leadership elite determined by school, university, birth or money is both a clear falsehood and of significant detriment to us all – denying, as it does, the benefits to society of more, better leaders. We especially need leaders from disadvantaged backgrounds, people who have the intelligence, skills and desire, but feel, through circumstance, that it will just never be them. We must also unlock the potential of those who already hold leadership positions, from teachers to politicians. We need to help people rethink how they lead, to shake off the waffle that gets in the way and enable them to be more successful through focusing on the aspects of leadership that matter most.

The demystification of leadership therefore becomes a powerful way to break down the barriers that inhibit people from fulfilling their potential as leaders and that exclude those who erroneously believe leadership is not something they can aspire to.

This book's ambition is to empower (sorry to use such a clichéd word, but here no other will do) as many as possible to take up their authority and lead. And to lead well, because great leadership, as well as being fantastically rewarding in and of itself, is a powerful force for the improvement of the lives of others. For many the

aspiration to be a leader can be the route to the realisation of their dreams and ambitions. Expensive education
and great exam results do not make great leaders. Yet
great leadership makes dreams come true, improves the
lives of those it touches and can liberate people from their
baggage – which we all carry. A great leader creates great
leaders and creates opportunities where none existed
before. The more we demystify leadership, the more
people will believe it can be them and the more people
will believe they can make a difference to the things that
matter most to them.

This, then, isn't a leadership book in the usual sense. It
isn't a book for those who simply want a pay rise. Rather
it is for those who want to get stuff done, for those who
have a dream they want to fulfil, for those who want to
fix things, help people, make things better, change stuff;
it's for the impatient and frustrated. A former colleague of
mine would ask, do you work for people less ambitious
than you? If you do, this is for you too.

Leadership is not a theoretical, academic subject, no
matter how many people try and make it such (and try to
separate you from your money in doing so). It is a craft,
and can only ultimately be honed through practice and by
failures of your own. Be eternally wary of those who claim
to be experts on the subject if they have only learned in a
classroom or by reading and regurgitating the words of
others. You would no more learn how to fly from somebody
who had never been in a cockpit than you should learn to
lead from one who has never walked in a leader's shoes. A
great leader is not a theorist, but a practitioner.

That all said, leadership is only one part of your life, only one of your dreams, and although it may be a route to their fulfilment it cannot be all-consuming or it will consume you. We are all more than one person, existing in more than one context; we are all workers, partners, bosses, siblings, parents and children. To lead you must be able to maintain each aspect of yourself in parallel with all the others, be able to switch off, walk away, relax – as well as get your game face on once Monday comes around.

I hope I have provoked you to think about leadership in a different way, a clearer way and a more practical way. However, ultimately this book can provide only the framework. You must bring the rest.

Finally, there is a beautiful line in *Middlemarch* by George Eliot, which encapsulates the huge role we little people play:

> *'The growing good of the world is partly dependent on unhistoric acts; and that things are not so ill with you and me as they might have been, is half owing to the number who lived faithfully a hidden life, and rest in unvisited tombs.'*

George Eliot herself of course lies far from forgotten or unvisited, but with my apologies, I have a small amendment: The growing good of the world is *mostly* dependent on unhistoric *leaders*. They are why things are not so ill with you and me as they might have been.

Millions can and do lead; millions more could if they were given and could grasp the chance. Were that to be the case it would be to the benefit of us all.

But enough of the bullshit, let's get on with it.

SELECTED FURTHER READING

Bishop, Gary John, *UnF*ck Yourself*
   A practical guide to sorting out your life

Blanchard, Ken, *The One Minute Manager*
   Very short, very no bullshit and very effective.
   A classic

Brearley, Mike, *On Form*
   A psychoanalyst's view on building winning teams.
   And much, much more

Duckworth, Angela, *Grit*
   Where I first came across the Will Smith quote in
   Chapter 6

Gawande, Atul, *The Checklist Manifesto*
   If this book is about getting things done, Gawande's
   is about getting things right. Every time

Harford, Tim, *Adapt: Why Success Always Starts
with Failure*
   A fascinating series of case studies about planning,
   failing, learning and trying again

Jacobs, Alan, *How to Think*
   Changed how I think

Kotter, John, *Our Iceberg Is Melting*

> A change management classic, but told as a children's story

Lewis, Michael, *The Undoing Project*

> A fascinating study on understanding how we decide (and surprisingly something of a tear-jerker)

Marcus Aurelius, *Meditations*

> Stoicism as interpreted by a Roman emperor